PREFACE

THE AIM OF the international soccer blog Pitch Invasion has been to publish thoughtful, long-form pieces of writing that dig well below the headlines, and explore the culture of sport, its politics, its economics and how fans engage with and shape the spectacles that dominate daily media coverage. This writing has come from a variety of contributors, and the very best of it from 2007 to 2010 is collected here. Though based out of Chicago, Pitch Invasion's focus has been global in scope. The breadth of topics explored by Pitch Invasion's writers has been remarkable, and selecting the essays for this volume proved to be a considerable challenge.

Categorizing the content helped. The first section, Fandom, looks at supporter culture in three continents. Mike Tuckerman and Mike Innes both explore Japanese fan culture, with the former offering a broad overview of how Japanese society lends to the formation of disciplined supporter groups, while the latter looks at the travails of Omiya Ardija's fans, the "Squirrel Nation." Across the Pacific, the American Northwest has recently become a hotbed for supporter engagement. Zach Dundas gives us the story of how the Timbers Army in Portland grew from grassroots to MLS; while Benjamin Kumming examines how DIY ethos and Major League marketing play out in a considered comparison of those same Portland fans with their noisy neighbors in Seattle. But where does this group mentality stem from? Andrew Guest dips into psychology to offer an explanation of the us-versus-them phenomenon. A study of social pathology might be needed in Poland, as Michał Karaś delves into a fierce Krakow rivalry.

History is also covered on three continents. Lost North American soccer is expansively explored by Kumming and Peter Wilt, both digging up the Dark Ages of American soccer – the interregnum between the demise of the NASL in 1984 and the launch of MLS in 1996. Richard Whittall reminds us of a little-known Canadian episode in Bobby Robson's long career, and my own piece on 1967 in American soccer considers the mess that the NASL formed out of. Africa is explored in three very different historical contexts. Supriya Nair warns us of the dangers of generalizations about sport and politics; Jack Lord goes back to the days of African football's development under colonial rule; and I consider the remarkable career of Ydnekatchew Tessema, a brilliant player, coach and most lastingly, a trailblazing promoter of African soccer internationally. JL Murtaugh, meanwhile, takes us to Europe with an analysis of the European Championship's brand identity since its inception in 1960.

Culture is a broad term, but fits for the essays by Brian Phillips, Jennifer Doyle and Vanda Wilcox on the curious origins of songs that have become supporter hymns in Bristol, London and Italy respectively. Alex Usher, Pitch Invasion's resident book reviewer, is represented with his rough guide to football books and with a particularly insightful look at Laurent Dubois' *Soccer Empire*. Eschewing the obvious comparison to the recent Zinedine Zidane film, Marc Bahnsen considers George Best on his own terms via the cameras trained on him in the German film from 1971, *Football as Never Before*.

The fourth section, Life, connects loss, love, hope and the commercialization of sport. Bobby Brandon calls for Robert Enke's tragic suicide to prompt an honest discussion about depression in sport. Two very different advocates of American soccer are remembered: punk-rock writer Steven Wells by myself, and Chicago Fire fan Al Hack by Peter Wilt. Each represented a different angle of the advance soccer has taken in the past two decades, from supporter culture to family life. How that passion for the sport can infect us is considered by David Keyes, who tells us how an American soccer neophyte became a fanatic with a trip to Saprissa in Costa Rica. Bahnsen returns to consider the commercialization that threatens international sport's organic appeal during Euro 2008, while Jennifer Doyle warns us of over-romanticizing sport's abilities to break down barriers.

Supporter activism closes the collection. How might fans engage to improve the sport they love? Dave Boyle, CEO of Supporters Direct from 2009-2011, examines what needs to change in English non-League football. His insights are well supported by Gary Andrews' series on the supporter trust movement, Shay Golub's look at Israeli fandom and Chris Taylor's consideration of club identity in non-League English football. And in Finland, Egan Richardson explores the challenges for activist fans.

The name Pitch Invasion aims to convey the passionate intensity with which fans form the culture of soccer worldwide. This is reflected in the depth and intensity of the topics collected here, and throughout Pitch Invasion's existence. I hope you enjoy this selection.

– *Tom Dunmore, Pitch Invasion Founder and Editor*

THE VERY BEST OF PITCH INVASION

pi

THE VERY BEST OF PITCH INVASION

21st Century Soccer Writing

EDITED BY TOM DUNMORE

PITCH INVASION PRESS | CHICAGO

pi

Pitch Invasion Press
Chicago, Illinois
United States of America
press@pitchinvasion.net
The very best of pitch invasion /
edited by Tom Dunmore
© 2011 Pitch Invasion Press

ISBN 978-0615546834

Design by Tom Dunmore
Cover photo by Josh Crockett

For all those who have read, written & commented
on Pitch Invasion since 2007.

CONTENTS

FANDOM

HISTORY

CULTURE

FANDOM

GROUP HARMONY

JAPAN'S FAN CULTURE

MIKE TUCKERMAN

AUGUST 20TH 2008

MUCH HAS BEEN written in English about the impact of professional football in Japan. The media's interest reached its peak in the run up to the 2002 FIFA World Cup, when two books in the form of Jonathan Birchall's *Ultra Nippon* and Sebastian Moffett's *Japanese Rules* hit the shelves.

Birchall's account of Shimizu S-Pulse's excruciating 1999 Championship Series playoff defeat to local rivals Júbilo Iwata is riveting. Yet his incredulous tone ultimately patronises S-Pulse fans and hints at the fact that Birchall is an interloper, with no prior knowledge of Japan and its culture.

Moffett's excellent *Japanese Rules* is a far more measured account, but the problem with both is that the books end with Japan co-hosting the World Cup in 2002. Coincidentally, that's about the time that the English-speaking world ceased to take an interest in the J. League, but much has changed since then. Step into any Japanese top flight stadium as an uninitiated fan now and the first thing that hits you is a wall of sound. Noisy support is de rigueur, and those who insist that J. League supporters are simply mimicking their counterparts in Europe and South America have clearly never attended a baseball game in Japan.

ORGANISED SUPPORT

From the multitude of unofficial fan clubs that crowd the terraces to the carefully choreographed chants that ring out for ninety minutes, J. League fans have arguably borrowed as heavily from their native baseball league as they have from European and South American football culture.

While baseball retains its image as a somewhat staid past-time in what is a relentlessly conservative country, football supporters in Japan broke the mould early, with Kashiwa Reysol fans setting the earliest trends for excessively passionate support.

Kashima Antlers' InFight were arguably the first well-organised fan club to travel the length of the country in support of their team, but these days it is Urawa's travelling hordes who continue to polarise opinion.

The Reds' story is a well-worn one of a struggling underdog come good, but in a country obsessed with glamour, the extra twenty thousand fans to have recently clambered aboard the Reds roller coaster have sparked claims that much of Urawa's support is made up of "plastic fans." Whether that is the cause of the inferiority complex that Urawa's more hard-core supporters lumber around with them is a mystery, but at any rate the most recent instances of fan violence have almost always involved the Reds.

Urawa fans deserve further scrutiny. At their best, Reds fans produce an atmosphere worthy of any match in the Bundesliga – from which the Saitama club borrowed heavily in the mid-1990s. Opposition teams are always greeted by a cacophony of noise, with hopeful away fans forced to up the ante to compete with the vociferous support raining down from the northern end of Saitama Stadium.

Yet Urawa's hardcore support has grown increasingly boor-ish. From the days of support-ing their team with relentless zeal at the dilapidated Komaba Stadium – which included a trip to the Second Division in 2000 – Urawa's support has not only been diluted by the move to the far larger Saitama Stadium, it has also become increasingly inane.

Instead of offering support to their team, many Urawa fans have simply taken to booing the oppo-sition, and a string of more than three opposition passes prompts a predictable chorus of jeers from the Urawa faithful.

There were more than a few wry smiles up and down the country, then, when Urawa inex-plicably choked away at relegated Yokohama FC on the final day last season, handing the title to bit-ter rivals Kashima Antlers in the process.

GROUP ORIENTATION

The organised nature of support in Japan is often misunderstood, and stands in glaring contrast to the spontaneous outbursts synonymous with English football. The word "fascist" pops up from time to time to describe J. League fans – not because of any particular right-wing political leanings, but rather due to the rigidly organised nature of their chants. That has given rise to claims from some Euro-versed analysts that J. League supporters are not in tune with the action on the pitch.

However, such criticism overlooks the fact that Japan remains a group-oriented society. While J. League stadia offer fans the chance to cast off the shackles of an overbearingly formal social structure, that fans choose to do so in unison with their fellow supporters should come as no surprise in a country where the concept of *wa* – or group harmony – is one of the central tenants of its culture.

Elaborately choreographed card displays are one aspect of European culture that have made their way onto J. League terraces, while the fact that hardcore fans stand at J. League grounds makes the giant flag display an old favourite. Uniquely Japanese are the team slogans, however, which routinely delight English-speaking fans with their Babelfish-inspired Engrish. Júbilo Iwata's "Hungrrrrry" invoked mirth from local rivals Shimizu S-Pulse this season, but the joke may be on S-Pulse for their "We Believe" slogan, with the club failing to inform fans to believe that a relegation dogfight was on the cards.

Supporter groups also adorn themselves with some inspired translations, with Kyoto Sanga fanclub "Real Naked" making a name for themselves as a group of men who support their team in bare chests – fortunately for them, the J. League is a summer-based competition.

Despite some of the more uniform aspects of J. League support, the match-day experience for all eighteen top-flight clubs differs from team to team. The 2002 World Cup may have left a legacy of international-class stadia, but it has proved problematic for some well-established clubs such as Nagoya Grampus, who alternate their fixtures between the ageing Mizuho Athletics Stadium in downtown Nagoya and the ultra-modern Toyota Stadium, situated some thirty-five kilometres out of town.

That's a situation mirrored across the league, with several top flight clubs regularly splitting fixtures between a variety of stadia. Given that clubs rent their grounds from local councils it has also led to some radical and unusual scheduling – with Kyoto Sanga "hosting" Yokohama F. Marinos hundreds of kilometres from the former imperial city in Kagoshima's Kamoike Stadium, while Gamba Osaka played the first leg of their League Cup quarter-final against the Marinos in distant Kanazawa.

LOST IN TRANSLATION

For Japan-based foreign fans, supporting a J. League club can be a hit-and-miss affair. Some clubs welcome foreign supporters with open arms. In the case of FC Tokyo – perhaps the only J. League club to have lifted its influences straight from British football – one highlight is the annual U.K. Day, where holders of a British passport are entitled to discount tickets and are treated to standard English fare inside Tokyo's cavernous Ajinomoto Stadium.

With matchday line-ups announced in English and a rousing rendition of "You'll Never Walk Alone" belted out before kick-off, there's no mistaking who FC Tokyo fans are paying homage to. Other clubs offer a nod to Japan's sizeable Brazilian community – arguably the largest minority group in what is practically a homogenous society – with the Auriverde always on display when Júbilo Iwata take to the pitch. Still, in a country that remains largely suspicious of foreigners, many J. League clubs simply prefer to ignore the smattering of foreign fans that dot the terraces on a weekly basis, offering little in the way of support for non-Japanese speaking fans.

The days of extra-time and penalty shoot-outs to decide drawn games are long gone, while the two-stage championship has also disappeared from view. The image of the J. League as a mere "retirement home" for ageing European stars is also an enduring, albeit unrealistic point of view, with the league having instead matured into a legitimate, sustainable competition.

Nevertheless, while the forces of modernity will invariably continue to thrust the J. League into a wider global context, there's no doubt that it remains a competition blessed with an alluring charm and a unique dose of East Asian exoticism. **pi**

DIY OR PREFAB?

PORTLAND, SEATTLE & SUCCESS IN

AMERICAN SOCCER CULTURE

BENJAMIN KUMMING

AUGUST 9TH 2009

On July 23RD 2010, the City Council of Portland, Oregon, approved a plan to renovate PGE Park, home of USL-1 side the Portland Timbers. The renovation and expansion of the long-time home of the Timbers was a point of contention – a necessity if the Timbers were to host MLS games at PGE Park, but one that required city financing. And so, as the mayor was paraded before the raucous Timbers Army, Portland's supporters' umbrella group, and the club-record 14,000 in attendance, fans rightfully celebrated their impending berth in North America's top-flight soccer league.

However, with the good news there will now come inevitable comparisons with the Timbers' primary rival, and MLS expansion case study, the nearby Seattle Sounders. And these comparisons make Timbers fans bristle. You see, while Seattle's inaugural MLS season has been an undoubted success, Portlanders are suffering through what amounts to a sporting version of the overlooked younger sibling. They have been toiling away in the deep darkness of USL soccer for years, growing one of the largest supporters' sections in any league in the United States, and all through grassroot organization. But in a few months of Seattle Sounders MLS soccer, Portland has been overshadowed by what is, by all accounts, MLS' most successful expansion to date.

HISTORIC RIVALRY

Soccer in the two cities shares a similar history, dating back to the mid-seventies halcyon years of the NASL. The Sounders and Timbers were admitted as expansion franchises in 1974 and 1975 and folded in 1982 and 1983 respectively, as the league disintegrated.

In the years after, as North American soccer died and was reborn and moved inside and back outside and died again, seemingly without end, teams from both cities competed in the alphabet soup of interim leagues, like the WSA, WSL, ASL and ASPL. It was not until the USSF firmly established the United Soccer Leagues and a federation-run pyramid that the teams found stability. In the USL A-League (the nation's top-flight until MLS was formed) the Seattle Sounders name and logo was rededicated in 1994, and the Timbers followed suit some seven years later in 2001.

In the A-League (later renamed USL First Division), Seattle proved to be a strong force, winning four League Championships and reaching U.S. Open Cup semi-finals three times. Portland, on the other hand, struggled mightily, never winning the league, or making it past the fourth round of the Open Cup. The Timbers' greatest success was winning the 2004 A-League Western Division.

Off the field, however, the results were reversed. Seattle struggled to attract crowds over 3,000 for their entire existence, averaging closer to 2,000 around the turn of the millennium. Their highest average attendance came in their inaugural A-League season, 1994, with an average of 6,347 fans per game. Otherwise, the average for their entire existence in the A-League/USL-1 was 3,194.

Compare that with the Timbers, who've averaged nearly twice that in their seven years of USL soccer: 6,235. In fact, in '07 and '08, the Timbers have been the second highest drawing team in USL, behind only Montreal (who miraculously draw well over 10,000 regularly because French Canada is just inexplicable). The Timbers also became considerably well ingrained into the city's sports consciousness, having only to compete with the NBA's Trailblazers and Triple-A baseball.

Crowning the large crowds (large by our modest standards, of course) is the Timbers Army, who occupy the North End of the stadium and have built a reputation for being among the most active supporters in any league in the United States – a recent "animated" tifo display, in which a 20-foot lumberjack clad in Timbers green chopped down a replica of the

Seattle Space Needle, made waves in the deep recesses of the internet reserved for American soccer talk.

GUERRILLA MARKETING

All of that work, though, and the Timbers Army's brick-by-brick construction of their club's identity, has been eclipsed by the sudden appearance of a soccer marketing giant to the north, where before there had been little comparison between the two.

Seattle Sounders FC is going gangbusters since their "promotion" to MLS this season, both on the field in MLS and in the stands (and in the bank and in the city and in the news). In contrast to their meager USL days, the MLS Sounders have drawn average crowds near 30,000 in their 10 home matches this season. Yes. 30,000. You read that correctly (the semi-official number is 29,983.90, but all those zeroes look better in print). You may be doing some quick math in your head right now, so I'll give you a moment to work it all out.

In the meantime, note that MLS' previous best-team-ever-everybody-look-at-that, Toronto FC, are averaging 20,277 (probably as a function of stadium capacity – they'd draw more if they could). Have you done the math yet? The MLS Sounders are drawing almost ten times as many fans than they did just last year, in the same stadium, with the same name. So what gives? Well, that's what the Timbers Army want to know when they chant "Where were you last year?!" at the seas of Sounders fans at Qwest Field.

A perfect storm settled over Seattle in 2008, at least as far as Seattle Sounders FC ownership group (faced by mascot Drew Carey but mainly backed by Hollywooder Joe Roth, along with Adrian Hanauer and Microsoft founder Paul Allen) were concerned. Seattle's oldest sports team, gridiron's Seattle Seahawks, were suffering a miserable season while winning only four games and missing the playoffs by a mile and a half. Baseball's Mariners had been nothing more than mediocre for some time. Most important, however, was the departure for Oklahoma City of the city's most successful and nationally renowned sports team, the NBA's SuperSonics. That left a huge gaping hole in Seattle's sports consciousness.

The Sounders plugged that hole with scarves. In a "guerilla marketing" maneuver, engineered by Seattle-based Wexley School for Girls (a jocularly named "alt" ad and marketing agency), thousands of Seattle Sounders FC branded scarves were disseminated around the metropolitan area and fans were encouraged to display them publicly in a Scarf Seattle campaign.

The maneuver worked, and the city's mailboxes, balconies, and shop windows were all a-flutter with the blue and green scarves. Through special offers to groups, Seahawks season ticket holders, and the like, the Sounders managed to sell 13,000 season tickets in a matter of weeks. While some of the announced tickets were actually Seahawks holders who had simply not yet passed up their special offer, the number created buzz, and the momentum kept the sales sky-rocketing. By season's start, there were nearly 20,000 legitimate Sounders season ticket holders. Throughout the city, posters, schedules and bar signs began popping up and a giant scarf was hung from a highway overpass. It was a perfect modern marketing gimmick: make the buzz, and the buzz makes sales, even if the product is totally unknown.

And therein lies the rub for the Timbers Army and their DIY culture down the road. Seattle's initial success was the result of expensive marketing. John Keatley's blog is an insider's look that innocently enough details a stage of the campaign in which, since there were no available press photos of Sounders fans, a cartoon modeling company was hired to make the background for a billboard. Tellingly, Portlanders refer to Sounders fans as "customers," characterizing them as simply having been the victims of good advertising. But the complaints go deeper than street-marketing.

DO IT YOURSELF

In the strange marketplace and cultural space of American soccer, the idea of authenticity has become vital to supporters and fans. Many fan groups around the country have struggled hard to develop an identity, often at odds with the management groups of their supported clubs that, in the early days, insisted on clean family-friendly atmospheres, hoping to cash in on the soccer-mom and youth team market. This has made the DIY ethic a point of pride for many North American supporters groups, who view the trials and tribulations of the past as battles won. For example, many supporter groups in MLS have had to make their own team merchandise and even large flags and banners, paid for out of association dues. The Timbers Army are perhaps the epitome of this sense of DIY pride, especially considering that they've labored in anonymity in the lower divisions. In many ways, to Timbers supporters, the sudden success of Seattle Sounders FC seems to represent the opposite of this mentality.

Meanwhile, within the stadium, Seattle's games are conducted under much pomp and circumstance – a marching band, the Sound Wave, marches with fans into the stadium prior to kick off, green and blue confetti is shot from cannons overhead as the team is announced, and canned music blares out of the PA throughout the proceedings. The stadium announcer reads a dramatic script in a (presumably authentic) posh English accent, not unlike Robin Leach of Lifestyles of the Rich and Famous.

And amidst all of this, fans hold aloft their uniform team-granted scarves. Overhead, large branded tarps cover unused seats in the top tier – a good use of dead space, except that one of them features goalkeeper Kevin Hartman, who plays for the Kansas City Wizards.

The whole ordeal feels as orchestrated as The Lion King On Ice. It is, without a doubt, a choreographed and controlled game experience – the antithesis to the anarchic, heady and wild experience so many supporters groups have struggled for so many years to engender in other stadia, not only in Portland, but also in Chicago, DC and other MLS markets. It's no wonder the Sounders Experience has been derided as plastic, prefabricated, and shallow.

That said, such derision is in some sense the product of envy. Seattle is what every American soccer team strives to be – appreciated by the city and treated as a sporting equal to other major sports, supported by regular sell out crowds, carried on local broadcast television, with a highly visible presence in the market. Seattle is strewn with Sounderphernalia, from team gear in the Space Needle gift shop to a branded Budweiser sign in every bar. Restaurants advertise televised games to draw customers. In most MLS cities, teams are lucky to have more than one "soccer bar" through which to market and build community, and it's rare one can find merchandise available anywhere but at the stadium.

Teams in MLS sit across an uncomfortable dichotomy: one at play in the Northwest, but representing the entire soccer culture – that between supporters (being those fans who participate regularly in supporters' sections, singing, displays of tifo and pyrotechnics and the like) and casual fans. The problem is that there simply are not enough supporters in any given American market to alone make a team profitable. Instead, much like the majority of attendees at an NBA or MLB game are not season ticket holding, chest painting, laid-off Ford plant workers, the casual fan has long been the holy grail for MLS. Drawing a group of 20,000 fans – diehard supporters or not – at each and every match is what will make MLS teams profitable, more pervasive in the sports consciousness, and permanent.

On the other hand, however, as in all sports it is the wildly zealous and colorful die-hard fans that generate a team's sense of identity and make the experience unique. You need only look to two-team baseball markets to find how the cultures of teams differ from club to club. Soccer's single biggest asset, the thing that makes it a unique sport experience (and thus a unique return on your entertainment dollar) is the supporters. No other sport in North America produces a similar fan environment to the supporters' sections in MLS from DC to Chicago to the newer expansion teams, not even close.

Thankfully, many soccer teams in the States are beginning to realize this, and are slowly undoing years of adversarial relations by trying to encourage the growth of supporters' sections. After all, while the moms and dads will be the largest paying group, none of them will pay as often and as repeatedly as the supporters, and none will broadcast the brand as fervently. The Timbers' highest attendance came in 2008, the year the team finished dead last in the table. These groups are the permanent kernel of the team's identity, which is absolutely vital to the survival of an underdog sport like soccer in America.

Of course, Qwest Field in Seattle is not exactly populated solely by Mariners fans who wandered into the wrong stadium. The Emerald City Supporters group was founded in 2005, back when the Sounders were a USL franchise. Still active today, the ECS has grown into an umbrella organization representing various supporters' clubs that occupy what has become known as the Brougham End, behind the southern goal. As do all other supporter groups, they organize tifo, stand, and sing, and just as Qwest Field is near capacity, the sections occupied by the ECS have been full for every MLS game – even if they get their tifo upside down upon occasion.

It is at the intersection of these two sectors where MLS pay dirt lays. For while ECS and Seattle's soccer-knowledgeable hardcore perhaps face an uphill battle to impart some personality on their squeaky clean new top-flight team, the Timbers Army will face a struggle to meld their raucous, foul mouthed energy with the family crowd the Timbers will need in MLS. In a recent interview in the *Oregonian*, Timbers owner Merritt Paulson saluted the Scarf Seattle campaign as a huge success, saying it will "go down in history as one of the all-time great marketing campaigns...that campaign, ultimately resulting in everybody bringing all the scarves to the games, was in my mind one of the great examples of brilliant marketing. And we may take elements of that."

It's no secret that the success in Seattle has made every MLS executive sit up and begin taking furious notes, hoping to glean some bit of knowledge or luck that will draw that elusive beast, the average American sports fan, out of its armchair. Portland will want him just as much Seattle does, as will Vancouver and Philly, and as does the frustrated bulk of MLS teams from floundering franchises like New York and Dallas to clubs on the cusp like Chicago, Houston and DC.

So while the Timbers Army can bemoan having been overlooked, and MLS fans can have a go at Seattle's preposterous game day fanfare and the newly minted fans with their team supplied scarves, Seattle is still out drawing all other MLS markets by a long shot. Here's the rub, and the moral that risks going unnoticed. The true goal of all MLS teams, Seattle and Portland included, should be a melding of these two approaches. After all, marketing puts asses in seats, but the atmosphere created by dedicated, Do-It-Yourselfing supporters, the thing that makes soccer unique against an increasingly noisy sports market, gets them to come back. Shooting confetti from cannons does not. **pi**

PORTLAND IN MLS

THE ORIGINS OF THE TIMBERS ARMY

ZACH DUNDAS

MARCH 20ᵀᴴ 2009

A S THEY SAY in other soccer countries, we're going up. Today, Major League Soccer commissioner Don Garber anointed the Portland Timbers – our modest local soccer team with the not-so-modest grassroots fan following, the Timbers Army – as the latest franchise in the nation's top soccer league.

Much has been said about the machinations behind the MLS expansion process: some informed criticism; some informed defense; much blather from the usual local know-nothings. Less has been said about what elevation to MLS means for the vibrant, homegrown micro-culture of the Timbers and the broader metropolitan culture of Portland. Leaving aside the gnarly financial and political details, the Timbers' rise caps a remarkable little episode in local

history, and begins a new one. For those of us who have followed the team, to one degree or another, since its modern-day launch in 2001, it's an emotional moment. Yes, we're going up. What does it mean?

SOCCER CITY USA

In *The Ball is Round*, his majestic global history of soccer, author David Goldblatt insists that a given football club – and, in a larger sense, football culture – grows out of the culture, economy, politics and identity of its city, nation and time. The tumultuous radicalism of "Red Vienna" in the 1920s birthed a cerebral style of play exemplified by Matthias Sindelar, who mocked the Nazis at Austria's final national team game before the *Anschluss*. The staggering number of pro clubs in Buenos Aires replicates the city's ethnic and political diversity and fierce neighborhood pride. Liberal, tolerant 1970s Holland directly informed that era's free-thinking, experimental Ajax and Dutch national sides. And the transformation of Premier League titans like Manchester United and Chelsea into "global brands" owned by foreign tycoons reflected the deregulated flow of capital, labor and information in the booms of the '90s and '00s.

So it goes with the Portland Timbers Football Club. Our team and the culture that surrounds it are both near-perfect reflections of the city circa now.

The original Timbers thrived in the middle and late 1970s, roughly coinciding with many of the crucial civic decisions that shaped modern Portland. The same era that gave us the urban-growth boundary, the beginnings of light rail and our identity as an environmental and subcultural Mecca gave us Pele's last game at Civic Stadium, Clive Charles and the faint but enduring nickname "Soccer City USA." The recession of the early '80s killed the first Timbers and the North American Soccer League itself, ensuring that football continued to subsist as a fringe sport in the US. Likewise, Portland itself faced economic malaise, and the payoff from the landmark decisions and cultural shifts of the '70s took a while to arrive.

The '80s and '90s saw a number of attempts to create a professional club in Portland, none of which stuck. Still, the football culture that began, more or less, with the original Timbers took root and evolved. Elite youth clubs and a vigorous high-school football scene honed generations of players. Huge participatory leagues grew up around both the outdoor game and the indoor vari-ant, and specialty shops opened to serve their equipment needs.

The University of Portland programs, under Charles' stew-ardship, achieved national renown and, by the standards of the collegiate game, healthy crowds. Nike's presence here attracted the North American headquarters of its main global competitor, Adidas. Adidas' extraordinary heritage as a foot-ball brand prompted Nike – long a tentative presence in the game – to master soccer's language and nuance, develop first-class product and move aggressively to snap up club, national and player endorsements.

Here and there, pubs showed European matches in the early morning or dead of night.

Portland changed. Hispanic, Asian and African communities arrived and flourished, as did a smaller but (at least for football culture) important stream of European expatriates, drawn by work at the sportswear brands, software companies or less quantifiable reasons. The American generations raised with soccer came of age, and at least a few didn't give up the game as a youthful pastime. Meanwhile, the city's music and art scenes thrived, emerging from Seattle's shadow to cut a distinct figure on the national scene. The '70s-era policies designed to encourage density, preserve farmland and highlight neighborhood character began to foster a very distinct urban character, one focused (rhetorically, if not always in practice) on cultural independence, localism and small-scale enterprise.

Portland was determined not to be a standard-issue American city. We didn't want to be Phoenix or Cleveland – Amsterdam seemed more our speed. We kept it weird. We were, in other words, perfect for football.

By the late '90s, few cities could match Portland as a friendly home for US national team matches. The 1999 Women's World Cup games at Civic Stadium drew huge and passionate crowds. It was only a matter of time before a true professional team arrived.

When the Timbers reappeared in the spring of 2001, the dot-com era was still alive, if not particularly well. Portland experienced its own version of tech-boom hysteria, with the orange scooters of Kozmo.com patrolling the streets to deliver gourmet ice cream and videos at a net loss. The nouveau Timbers shared a little of the They-Do-It-With-Mirrors! character of all those strangely named, purposeless companies sucking up venture capital at the time.

The franchise ownership group put up a shiny façade, including a renovated and renamed PGE Park (in honor of an Enron subsidiary, no less), to conceal a flimsy, hyped-up business construct. I remember sitting, as a reporter, in a meeting in which I was shown an artist's rendering of a future pro gridiron football game at PGE – an XFL game. The stadium remodel managed to combine a not-very-good soccer park with a not-very-good baseball park, but did include a swish new sports bar.

And even though the Timbers would play in the second-tier USL, you could say the effort to educate the public on the difference between that circuit and MLS was less than diligent. (In fairness, MLS was wobbly at best at the time. No one would have been surprised if the thing had expired, leaving the USL on top of a very short pyramid.)

True to the era, the first owners eventually ran out of happy talk, found themselves afoul of financial commitments to their landlord and ostensible partners, the City of Portland, and departed the scene.

On the other hand, the team itself exuded an agreeable, wacky vibe. When I interviewed the supposed star signing, ex-MLS (and ex-everything else) player Darren Sawatzky, he met me for a cocktail at the Driftwood Room in the old Mallory Hotel. He brought along his brother, whom I believe was working concessions at PGE.

The general manager, a full-bore football fanatic named Jim Taylor, would have sent his cobbled-together side of kids, journeymen and semi-pros out against Arsenal in half a heartbeat, such was his enthusiasm. The head coach, an old school ex-West Ham man named Bobby Howe, was straight from Central Casting. I recall a concerted effort to turn the "lads" into gossip-column sex symbols. The team also boasted perhaps the greatest mascot in sports history: Timber Jim; a man in Carhartts; a man with a chainsaw; a man who sliced a hunk of wood off a log every time the Timbers scored and brandished it at rival goalkeepers in a threatening manner. Timber Jim added a jolt of deranged American genius to the Europhile world of soccer fandom.

Add a string section and voila: musical comedy. Still, it was football, and Portland was ready. The new Timbers' debut drew well over 10,000 fans, a terrific crowd in the context of the threadbare USL, better than many MLS attendances, and no doubt a shock to the chorus of dinosaur mainstream sports pundits who dismissed the new franchise in advance. (Taylor, I remember, was practically vibrating with excitement afterwards.) The germ of the Timbers Army hid somewhere in that opening night crowd inflated by curiosity-seekers and one-time fans. By the middle of that first season, the pioneer hardcores staked out Section 107, at the north end of the ground, as their turf. The first drums, horns and hand-painted banners began to appear.

BUILDING AN ARMY

In those early days, the Timbers Army consisted of a few punk rockers, some lifelong soccer nerds, the occasional Hispanic dude, a smattering of Portland's skins/ska/scooters contingent and whatever friends, acquaintances and significant others the afore-mentioned could drag along.

But Portland is a city where a small number of people can touch off a sizeable cultural wave, and from the beginning the Army possessed out-of-scale enterprise and energy. Various online efforts soon coalesced around the roiling Talk Timbers message board, and the Army developed a recruitment policy that would do either the real Army or the Lesbian Avengers proud.

With the terror attacks of 11 September 2001, the Bush Era began in earnest. The Timbers Army made its own small state-ment, displaying flags represent-ing all the players' nationalities (even Kyrgyzstan, I believe) at the first game after the tragedy. It was an early sign that the Army would become a bastion of a certain kind of resistance – not overtly political, since the leaderless, structureless Army undoubtedly takes in anarchists, Republicans, professional Democratic Party activists, Pacific Greens and people who don't vote.

But during the bizarre years that followed, with so much of the national discourse synthesized and choreographed, the Army functioned as a spontaneous outlet for authentic grassroots expression in a city that some-times felt like an internal-exile camp for liberals. And, if noth-ing else, the Timbers provided a forum in which to drink and forget.

In subtle ways, the fabric of the city itself helped the Army grow and Timbers survive. Unlike the average American stadium surrounded by oceanic parking lots, PGE Park sits amid a dense weave of streets and light-rail lines. Burnside Street, the central city's greasy main artery, pulses right past the stadium, lined by bars, restaurants and cafes.

The handy proximity of pubs like the Bitter End and the Bull Pen gives fans a chance to con-gregate before and after games, a crucial ingredient to the Army's attempt to create a European-style matchday culture. The fact that Timbers players – a blue-collar, underpaid breed – sometimes drop by for a post-game pint adds a unique flavor to the club.

As heroic Timbers defender Scot "With One 'T'" Thompson once noted, it doesn't happen in Los Angeles.

While all this feels organic and natural, the density, diversity and locally focused commerce around PGE Park are dividends of Portland's concerted political efforts to turn back urban decline. A visit to one of the sterile exurban stadiums built by MLS teams in recent years underlines the distinct character of the Timbers' environs.

While the club itself clung to viability under absentee ownership – enjoying, for a time, the dubious distinction of being the only football club in world history owned by a pro baseball league – the Army thrived. The fans shared a character-building history. Those of us who witnessed Chugger Adair, a forward with the monolithic stature (and mobility) of an Easter Island totem, will never forget him. On the field, the Timbers have won – to borrow an apt British-ism – sweet fuck all. In the stands, the club is arguably the most dynamic phenomenon in North American football culture. The evolution and internal nuance of Timbers Army culture could fuel many master's degree theses. Let it suffice to say that the spectacle of today's Army, which often numbers more than 1,000 fans packed into a surreal, maniacal, Technicolor-green north end, amazes me. The Army embodies Portland's eccentricity, creativity and DIY spirit, as well as an urban patriotism worthy of a medieval city-state. Major League Soccer has only a faint notion of the monster it is about to absorb.

And in the face of competitive struggles, perennial fiscal uncertainty and the utter obscurity of the USL, the Timbers also garnered a broader following. Attendance last year increased 25 percent over 2007 despite the team's hideous performance. (How hideous? Try 26 goals scored in 30 league games.) Within the USL First Division, only the Montreal Impact enjoyed stronger support. Fans in other parts of PGE Park generally appreciate the Army's boisterous shenanigans – an appreciation not always mutual, unfortunately. They also demonstrate Portland's larger appetite for cultural adventure. Though the city certainly harbors its own xenophobes, moron soccer-bashers and people who just can't be bothered to find out about something new, the average Portlander exhibits a commendable open-mindedness.

As the club joins MLS, this audience, which a personal ad might describe as "football-curious," will be the crucial factor in its success.

GOING UP

It now looks like the Timbers will last exactly 10 seasons in their USL incarnation. The club will then strip down and rebuild as an MLS franchise, keeping the treasured identity first forged in the swingin' '70s but changing just about everything else. The vitalizing, hate-charged rivalries with Seattle and Vancouver will migrate, too.

Instead of the Rochester Raging Rhinos, Puerto Rico Islanders and Carolina RailHawks, the fixture list will include the Los Angeles Galaxy, Houston Dynamo and DC United. International matches against Mexican and Central American teams beckon – and maybe MLS clubs really will play in South America's Copa Libertadores one day. Timbers v. Boca Juniors? It could happen, and PGE Park could become one of the best football venues on the continent.

Think what you will about the politicking that brings us here, this is going to be fun. The only question is whether the MLS-certified Timbers can maintain the fizzy underground brio of today's lo-fi club. That is a question that will largely be answered on the terraces instead of on the field. **pi**

LOVE, REVOLUTION & ARCHITECTURE

A YEAR IN THE LIFE OF THE SQUIRREL NATION

PART ONE

MIKE INNES

DECEMBER 13TH 2008

THE DERBY

THERE'S HALF AN hour to go before kick-off. Away behind one goal, a huddled group of fans dressed in orange strike up a chant, trying to ignore the torrential sheeting rain and the fact that a good half of the seats around them are empty. Some of the soaked supporters wave home-made banners upon which they've painstakingly transcribed the names of their favourite players and, despite the unpromising conditions, they do a decent job of making some noise, creating an atmosphere and a sense of anticipation ahead of this, the first derby game of the 2007 season.

Their goal-shy team might not have much of a chance in the match ahead. Recent results are hopelessly poor and the side is already in the relegation zone. Even so, the fans will do their best to encourage the team.

This, after all, is why many of them wear orange replica shirts sporting the number twelve: collectively, they play the role of the twelfth man and their job is to support the team all the way up to the final whistle. Who knows, maybe today there will be an incredible upset?

The response of the supporters in red behind the other goal – and indeed across most of the rest of the stadium, although they are nominally the away side today – seems explicitly designed to crush any such optimism stone dead. There is a shattering, physical volume, coordinated by nominated leaders with military precision, drums and voices united in the absolute certainty that their team of choice is the strongest in the land.

For Urawa Reds were champions of Japan in 2006 and are top of the league again today. They have a fanbase that stretches far beyond their home in Saitama prefecture, from Hokkaido in the north to Kyushu in the south.

They have the biggest budget and the best players and it is unthinkable that their diminutive near neighbours Omiya Ardija – the Squirrels, for God's sake – might today be in with even a sniff of a chance of avoiding an absolute hammering.

The Reds fans have home-made flags, too. One of them shows a large cartoon fist coming down from the sky, like a Monty Python foot, to crush an Ardija logo. Another features a squirrel being tossed into a garbage can, while a third simply bears the legend OMIYA FUCK.

When Omiya's mascot, a cheery seven-foot tall squirrel named Ardy, goes on a pre-match walkabout, the air is filled with catcalls, whistles and boos.

As kick-off time approaches, the regimented noise from the Urawa followers becomes if anything yet more intense. The supporters wearing orange,

meanwhile, continue to wave their banners and shake their umbrellas. You can see that they're still singing as well. You just can't hear them.

THE SQUIRREL NATION

Let's get the whole issue of the name out of the way first. Omiya itself is a small city in Saitama prefecture in central Japan and Ardija is a corruption of the Spanish word 'ardilla', which means 'squirrel', which is in turn a symbol of Omiya city. Expecting to understand Japanese football club names – Consadole Sapporo, say, or non-League outfit Renofa Yamaguchi – to any greater extent than that is like expecting to understand the deepest mysteries of the universe, so it's really best if you can just let it go there.

At least among the small pocket of foreign followers of teams in Japan's professional league, the J-League, Omiya Ardija supporters have as a consequence of all this picked up the nickname of the Squirrel Nation.

The passion which the Squirrel Nation feel for their diminutive club is something that has, as we shall see, grown greater than ever during the course of a tempestuous 2007, but in terms of the relationship with their near neighbours – the cities of Urawa and Omiya are a matter of only five miles apart – being regarded as playing second string is actually a pretty normal state of affairs for Ardija supporters.

The fact of the matter is that Urawa are far and away the most popular club in Japan, never mind on their own patch, and as such provide a straightforward default option for any new supporter getting into the game and hunting round for a team to follow. Manchester United is now and always has been a clear model for the Reds, from the cultural omnipresence to the design of the uniforms; even their proper full name is **Mitsubishi Urawa Football Club** (MUFC).

While Urawa can stage matches at the Saitama Stadium enormodome and turn it into a pulsating cauldron of noise populated by at least 40,000 followers chanting in tight unison, when Omiya play at the same venue they're satisfied to pull in a quarter of that number. And while Urawa aspire to being part of world football's upper echelons – they were thrilled at winning the Asian Champions League 2007, not particularly because it meant that they were better than other clubs in Asia, but more because it gave them an opportunity to match themselves up with top European and South American sides in the FIFA Club World Cup – Ardija operate under their noses at a local level, scrapping for every supporter they can get.

Perhaps not surprisingly, this means that the Squirrel Nation are a tightly-knit bunch, vociferous in their expression of the fact that there are most emphatically two teams in Saitama: a point consistently misunderstood by almost everyone who is not connected to the club. The mayor of Saitama City, for instance, making a speech at Omiya's brand new stadium and clad in an ill-fitting orange shirt, misjudged his audience as only a local politician can when, to a distinctly frosty response, he referred in glowing terms to the Reds and their recent achievements.

OMIYA PARK

Like almost all J-League teams, Omiya Ardija has their roots in the corporate football which blossomed across Japan in the '60s and '70s. While Urawa grew out of a Mitsubishi works side, Omiya's origins lie in a local representative team of the NTT telecommunications giant. NTT Kanto played Regional League football before gaining promotion to the lower ranks of the Japan Soccer League, a nationwide competition populated by company teams like Toshiba and Yamaha.

During the '90s, however, Japanese club football was changed beyond all recognition by the establishment of the J-League and in 1999 NTT rode the wave of sides joining the ranks of the professionals by being among the founder members of the second tier, J2. The team name was changed in accordance with J-League policy that clubs abandon their corporate monikers completely and instead choose something that grounded them in their local community.

In their first few seasons in J2, Omiya Ardija was mainly stuck in mid-table alongside other small teams, such as Montedio Yamagata and Sagan Tosu. The Squirrels nevertheless had one significant asset at their disposal, in that they were able to use as their home stadium Omiya Park, which prior to the World Cup of 2002 was one of the few football-specific stadia in Japan. Built to stage the football tournament of the 1964 Tokyo Olympics, the ground had a capacity of 12,000 and the lack of a running track gave it the kind of intimacy that meant a 5,000 crowd for a night game was enough to create a piping hot atmosphere. Despite the fact that Ardija were really no more than J2 also-rans, their stadium quickly developed a reputation among J-League fans as one of the best places to watch football in the whole country.

Late in 2004, however, a major problem arose from an unexpected source: suddenly, Omiya got good. In the final quarter of the lengthy J2 season, Squirrels coach Toshiya Miura somehow managed to coax a series of increasingly impressive performances from his squad and it was Ardija who emerged from the pack to move into second spot behind runaway leaders Kawasaki Frontale. In the end, Omiya notched up a remarkable thirteen-match winning streak to close out the year and thereby claim an incredible promotion.

Appropriately, the move up to J1 was finally confirmed at Omiya Park with a 3-1 defeat of Mito Hollyhock, after which players and fans celebrated together the club's shock success. Tears streamed down the face of Japanese-American midfielder Jun Marques

Davidson as he shook hands with Squirrels supporters: university students and high school girls, middle-aged salarymen, parents and little kids, all in their orange replica shirts. None of them could have dreamed that a tiny club like Ardija – boasting an average gate of barely 6,000 – would fight their way to a place among the elite of the Japanese game, alongside even their Saitama rivals the Reds.

But the problem for Ardija lay in the shape of their cosy, familiar old home stadium. Constructed in the leafy surrounds of the city's main park and with cherry trees shedding their blossom on the flag-waving fans behind the goal in the spring time, however charming it was, the fact remained that the venue was now showing its age. More to the point, it wasn't actually large enough for the 15,000 minimum capacity restriction placed by the J-League on stadia regularly staging J1 matches.

The Squirrels were subsequently allowed by league authorities to play a limited number of games there in the 2005 J1 season, but after a 1-0 win over Gamba Osaka in November of that year, the demolition men moved in and the stadium was completely knocked down.

It was estimated that construction of its replacement on the same site would take two years. Just at the very point that they were trying to establish themselves in the top division, Ardija were homeless. **pi**

LOVE, REVOLUTION & ARCHITECTURE

A YEAR IN THE LIFE OF THE SQUIRREL NATION

PART TWO

MIKE INNES

DECEMBER 17ᵀᴴ 2008

A YEAR IN THE LIFE

Tʜʀᴏᴜɢʜᴏᴜᴛ 2006 ᴀɴᴅ 2007, then, the majority of Omiya home fixtures were played at Komaba Stadium, a charmless concrete bowl complete with an athletics track. The Squirrel Nation hated the place. It was a 25 minute fun-filled walk from the nearest train station, for one thing. And it was located in Urawa.

Oh, and it just so happened to be something akin to the Reds' spiritual home. In contrast to Omiya Park, the small crowds attending Ardija games at Komaba found it almost impossible to generate a proper atmosphere and the hardcore support, instead of being able to reach out and touch the goalnets as they had been used to, were now fifty yards from the action.

But an additional factor was serving to isolate fans from the club. While few would have expected it to be easy to compete alongside teams of the stature of Urawa, Yokohama F. Marinos or Kashima Antlers, among Omiya supporters there nevertheless existed the feeling that their team had been underperforming and, for many, the root cause of this sense of potential unfulfilled lay in the club's transfer policy.

Time and again, foreign strikers in particular came to Omiya, failed to make any impact and were quietly let go. On other occasions, the Squirrels got rid of players who immediately went on to achieve terrific success at rival J-League clubs. Holder nominally of the position of Chief Scout, the man responsible for all this was Satoru Sakuma, effectively the General Manager of the club in that he oversaw the relationship with – and indeed continued to be employed by – main sponsor NTT. It was a mess and a constant source of dissatisfaction amongst supporters mistrustful of Sakuma's power and suspicious of the fact that he was not even employed by the football club.

2007 started, then, with Omiya Ardija in an uncomfortable position both off and on the pitch. Toshiya Miura had departed after three years as coach, having taken the team to promotion but then not having been able to move things up to the next level via his particularly cautious brand of football. Rumours abounded of the transfer budget having been blown the previous year, meaning that the incoming coach, inexperienced Dutchman Robert Verbeek, had little or no money to spend – or rather, to have Sakuma spend for him. The squad appeared notably weaker than 2006 and a relegation battle looked to be on the cards.

Defeats in all of the first four matches in March brought home what a tough year lay ahead. The team appeared ill-focused, with even less of a cutting edge than had been the case under Miura – and although the defence did begin to tighten up as new import

Leandro settled in alongside Daisuke Tomita in the middle of the back four, the Squirrels were scoring on average only once every two games. Worse was to come at the end of April, when the team put in a particularly feeble performance in a home defeat by Ventforet Kofu, one of the few J1 clubs who are actually a smaller concern than Omiya.

After the final whistle, for the first time fans staged a noisy protest calling for the dismissal not of coach Verbeek, but of Satoru Sakuma. It was plain to see, they argued, whose fault all this was: not so much the lifeless football and the dreadful results but the sheer energy-sapping lack of ambition that seemed to be pervading Omiya Ardija, the apparent belief that simply being in the top division was going to be sufficient for the supporters and really ought to provide satisfaction in itself.

Nothing, of course, changed. In fact, although the simmering resentment against Sakuma remained, this heralded a modest improvement in the team's fortunes. A hard-fought 1-1 draw in the rain at Saitama Stadium against high-flying Urawa turned out to be the first match of an eight-game unbeaten run.

But it was difficult to move up the standings when no fewer than four of those games were 0-0 draws and, as the season reached its mid-point in late June, there was an air of deep despondency enveloping the club: an unloved temporary home ground, third bottom in the league, lacklustre performances from players seemingly unconvinced by the new coach, very few goals scored and overseeing it all, Sakuma. How could things be much worse than this?

SAKUMA YAMERO!

A break in the match schedule saw the Squirrels squad on a training camp in order to prepare for the second half of the season. Just prior to the recommencement of the J1 calendar, Omiya staged a friendly against Urawa and while the Reds' line-up was filled with youngsters and fringe squad members, Robert Verbeek fielded more or less a full-strength side. The intention was that the Ardija players should use that match to put into practice the style of play and tactics that had been worked on during the camp, as a springboard for moving up the table.

The Squirrels had one shot throughout the whole of the ninety minutes and lost 6-0. They were shapeless, clearly uncommitted and ended up being torn apart by the young Urawa side. Verbeek was sacked later that evening.

The supporters were split regarding the wisdom of dismissing the Dutchman, some feeling that he'd done his best operating under difficult circumstances, while others took the view that his ultra-defensive approach was only ever going to achieve results by boring the opposition into submission. But there was to be no such disagreement when the identity of the new coach became clear.

To the horror of the Squirrel Nation and with just days to go before the re-start of J1 against a strong Shimizu S-Pulse team, it was quickly announced that Verbeek's replacement would be none other than Satoru Sakuma.

This was comedy gold for the sports press – who immediately nicknamed the new incumbent the "salaryman coach" – but total humiliation for the fans. As far as they were concerned, Sakuma had proved himself on countless occasions to be an appalling judge of players, he didn't even have any real coaching experience at all and was, even worse, still to be an employee of NTT rather than coming onto the payroll of Omiya Ardija.

The club talked about how imperative it was to remain in J1 – that they were under additional pressure from sponsors and from the local council, as the financial backers for the new stadium. But how, fans wondered, would it be possible for the team to make desperately-needed improvements under a coach who was in reality an office worker, a jobbing member of company staff? The Sakuma appointment seemed instead to represent a one-way ticket back to J2. The redeveloped Omiya Park would surely play host not to top flight football, but to the minnows of the Japanese pro game.

THE END

Luckily for Satoru Sakuma, in his first game in charge, Shimizu S-Pulse were way off form. Omiya scraped a 2-2 draw – only the second time all year that they had scored more than once in a match. The following week, though, Ardija were outclassed at home by Vissel Kobe before then being put to the sword by Kashima Antlers with what was a truly atrocious display.

The Squirrel Nation were aghast at how low their team had sunk. The players were uncoordinated and uncommitted – something it would never have been possible to say about Omiya sides of old – and the new coach was nothing but an incompetent with a giant ego.

Protests by the supporters would clearly have no effect, given that Sakuma was now running the show entirely and there was no desire amongst Omiya followers to undermine the confidence of the players yet further by wholesale booing of their increasingly woeful efforts.

But the fans' websites crackled with impotent fury, while those Ardija players who maintained inevitably anodyne blogs as part of their media profile found that, via the comments sections of their sites, they were on the receiving end of a level of anger that surprised even the fans themselves.

On the pitch, matters reached a head one Saturday at the end of August, when Omiya travelled to take on a Nagoya Grampus 8 side on a terrible run of results and further weakened by injury and suspension. If ever there was an opportunity for Sakuma's team to break out of their slump, this was it.

Omiya were crushed, 5-0. "The Squirrels followers who made the trip to Nagoya received for their effort and commitment nothing but mockery from the players," read one fansite after the match. The mother of two young supporters commented on the blog of captain Chikara Fujimoto that she didn't want her sons watching such awful football again, because it had made them cry. "Despair; thanks!" was the ironic posting of another fan on star midfielder Daigo Kobayashi's web diary.

But amongst all the animated online discussions, a point that came up again and again was perhaps best summed up by one blog writer when he remarked, "I never realised before now how much I love the club. This situation has brought it home just how much it means to me."

The players seemed to be performing if anything even more poorly since the appointment of Sakuma, but for the Squirrel Nation a sea change had occurred in their attitude to and relationship with the club. The mood was paradoxically buoyant. The players might not look as if they care, the thinking seemed to go, but it's our *job* to care: we're Omiya Ardija supporters and we can't change now.

All that was needed was for the team to provide a win. Any win. With ten or a dozen games to go there was still the possibility of avoiding relegation, but something needed to happen to kickstart a Squirrels revival. Incredibly, it came in the Saitama derby at the start of September when, with the score at 0-0 after an hour, league leaders Urawa had their defence sliced open. Forward Hiroshi Morita latched on to a perfectly weighted through ball after a surging run from the back by defender Leandro and clipped it past Reds keeper Ryota Tsuzuki for a hysterically celebrated goal.

The reigning champions pushed Omiya back to try and grab an equaliser, but found themselves matched up against an opponent who had discovered a resilience not seen all year long. Leandro and Tomita were disciplined in the heart of the defence and goalkeeper Koji Ezumi played with an assurance that seemed to unnerve the Urawa attack. Ardija held on, reasonably comfortably in the end, for a 1-0 win. Was there hope still for the rest of the season? **pi**

LOVE, REVOLUTION & ARCHITECTURE

A YEAR IN THE LIFE OF THE SQUIRREL NATION

PART THREE

MIKE INNES

JANUARY 8ᵀᴴ 2009

Built at a cost of some 400 million yen – much of which was paid by the local council – the rebuilt Omiya Park has a capacity of 15,000, similar to Shimizu S-Pulse's Nihondaira ground, with four separate stands built tight to the pitch. In contrast to the direction in which football stadium design is moving in certain other countries, it is not an all-seater venue in that the stands behind each goal feature terracing at the front and seats at the back. The only roof is down one side over the main stand, another particularly striking feature being the colossal hairdryer-style floodlights.

For the Squirrel Nation, it was their new home. The official opening game of the NACK 5 Stadium Omiya – retitled following a sponsorship deal with a local radio station – took place in early November, when with just four rounds to go in the 2007 J1 season, Ardija hosted Oita Trinita. It could scarcely have been a more delicately balanced fixture: a crucial relegation six-pointer, in which both sides knew that a win would see them take a giant stride towards safety.

The place was packed, each stand a sea of orange and blue. The scene was set for arguably the biggest day in the club's history and just three minutes in, midfielder Yoshiyuki Kobayashi grabbed the headlines as he took advantage of sloppy Oita defending to fire in the opening goal from twenty yards.

After such a stunning start, though, Omiya dithered and allowed the visitors back into the match. It was no surprise when

Yuki Fukaya tapped in a close-range equaliser midway through the first half and Omiya's coach Satoru Sakuma appeared content to concede the initiative altogether with his tactical changes, even as the match stood at one goal apiece. Ardija had a few half-chances after the interval, but the home side was usually second best. Sure enough, four minutes from time, Trinita forward Shunsuke Maeda scored the winner from close range.

The Squirrels had blown it. Oita took back with them to Kyushu three priceless points in the fight against the drop; Omiya were still deep in trouble and had lost the first match at their beautiful new ground in front of 15,000 fans. "The stadium's a palace," wrote one despondent member of the Squirrel Nation afterwards, "It's too good for this Omiya team."

THE FINAL COUNTDOWN: THREE

All across Japan, there are twenty three minutes to go in the penultimate round of fixtures in the 2007 J1 season. At a heaving Saitama Stadium, Urawa Reds have moments before gone a goal down in the top of the table crunch match with improving Kashima Antlers. Elsewhere, two teams are fighting to avoid the drop – hopelessly out of form and now in the relegation play-off spot, Sanfrecce Hiroshima trail 3-0 at Kawasaki Frontale, while just above them on goal difference, our Omiya Ardija are tied at 1-1 against FC Tokyo.

The preceding weeks had seen Omiya claw their way out of the relegation places. A handful of draws, that sensational 1-0 win over Urawa in the return derby match and a couple of narrow defeats of other struggling sides have seen Sakuma's side give themselves a chance of staying up.

The last few games have felt to the Squirrel Nation as if the team were playing on a knife edge, but unbelievably, with closest rivals Hiroshima three behind to Kawasaki, a victory over Tokyo would see Ardija practically guaranteed survival and J1 football at Omiya Park next year.

It's just that coach Sakuma doesn't seem to have realised this. Going for three points is the last thing on his mind: both strikers have been substituted, the Squirrels are playing 4-6-0 and are inviting the opposition to put them under pressure.

It looks almost as if it's willful, with Sakuma's baffling refusal to acknowledge that an attacking approach against a mid-table side with nothing to play for might yield dramatic results. And Tokyo midfielder and goalscorer Naohiro Ishikawa gathers the ball wide on the right, preparing to launch another attack.

THE FINAL COUNTDOWN: TWO

There's a minute on the clock now. Reds are still losing, as Kashima – playing with only nine men after two red cards – threaten to blow the title race wide open with what would be a sensational victory. Tokyo continue to press forward against Omiya, even though Sakuma has finally succumbed to reason and thrown on a striker: the injury-prone Naoto Sakurai, who hasn't scored a single goal all year. Kawasaki continue their stroll to victory over a shattered and demoralised Sanfrecce side.

For this is turning into merely the latest in a string of defeats for Hiroshima, in what has been a disastrous second half of the season. Boasting what is on paper one of the most dangerous front pairings in the country in veteran Brazilian goal machine Ueslei and his razor sharp foil Japanese

international Hisato Sato, fans can't grasp why results are so poor. But the fact is that due to a total collapse of form, coach Mihailo Petrovic's Sanfrecce side have picked up just two points from the last 24 and have plummeted down the standings to their current position.

With Ardija's game at Tokyo petering out to a 1-1 draw, Sanfrecce Hiroshima will go into the final match of the year knowing they need to beat third-placed Gamba Osaka, while relying at the same time on Kawasaki to get at least a point at Omiya. Difficult, yes, but – with Ueslei and Sato on board – maybe not quite impossible. They're still in with a chance. It's not over yet.

THE FINAL COUNTDOWN: ONE

Thirty seconds to go. The Red Army urge their team onwards, but the game looks to be up for them today; to retain the title, Urawa will just have to win at relegated Yokohama FC next week instead. Still three down in their match, Sanfrecce's thoughts have by now also turned to their next match against Gamba, while another FC Tokyo attack has just broken down against Ardija:

Omiya's Leandro picks up the ball just outside his own area and brings it away from danger.

He advances forward into space, the Tokyo forwards slow to track back alongside him. Brushing off a challenge, the big defender exchanges a swift one-two with Daigo Kobayashi that takes out another couple of opponents and sees him across the halfway line. Leandro doesn't have that much speed, but what he does have is power and momentum. This is enough to take him away from Tokyo's Ryoichi Kurisawa and by the time Masahiko Inoha tries to get close enough to the ball to make a challenge, all of a sudden Leandro is barely thirty yards from goal. The whole of the home side's defence has opened up before him.

Inoha has other ideas. Racing alongside his giant opponent and by this time desperate not to concede a free-kick or worse, with one lunge he makes a vital play for the ball. But Inoha's touch is weak; aiming to flick it out for a corner, the Tokyo man simply nudges it further on and Leandro takes it in his stride, now clean through on the goalkeeper. Exposed, Hitoshi Shiota seems caught in no man's land, backing off and then edging tentatively forwards to meet the onrushing Brazilian, but Leandro, now twelve yards out and unstoppable, makes up Shiota's mind for him as he crashes the ball over the keeper's shoulder and into the back of the net.

It's 2-1. He's actually scored. Leandro ran the entire length of the pitch and he scored. Omiya are winning. In the space of twelve seconds, one player has saved their season. The area of the stadium reserved for away fans is transformed into a mass of shrieking, orange-afro-wearing pandemonium, as the Squirrel Nation leap up and down, high-fiving and screaming at each other uncontrollably.

The players mob their teammate and Satoru Sakuma is caught on camera looking to the heavens, covering his face with his hands in a kind of ecstatic disbelief.

THE FINAL COUNTDOWN: ZERO (POSTSCRIPT)

In the last fixtures of the 2007 season, Omiya Ardija drew 1-1 with Kawasaki Frontale and Sanfrecce Hiroshima drew with Gamba Osaka. The Squirrels' place in J1 for 2008 was therefore confirmed as being safe and a few days later, Satoru Sakuma stood down as Ardija coach.

Sakuma's replacement was announced as being Yasuhiro Higuchi, who had in 2006 and 2007 led Montedio Yamagata to bottom-half-of-the-table finishes in J2. Hiroshima subsequently participated in the relegation play-off, which they lost 2-1 on aggregate to Kyoto Sanga. Urawa Reds lost 1-0 to Yokohama FC, a sensational defeat that allowed Kashima Antlers to pip them for the league title via a 3-0 defeat of Shimizu S-Pulse.

And so ended a rollercoaster J1 season, one the Squirrel Nation will not soon forget. **pi**

Another Postscript: In the seasons since this article was written the Squirrels have finished in 12th, 13th and 12th positions. At the time of writing they are in 15th place. Satoru Sakuma, who took up the post of General Manager at Ventforet Kofu, has recently sacked the club's coach and taken over himself; Ventforet are one place behind Ardija in J1. The whereabouts of Robert Verbeek are unknown.

THE HOLY WAR IN POLAND

MICHAŁ KARAŚ

MAY 6TH 2008

THE CENTENARY OF
THE HOLY WAR

ITS FULL NAME is the "Great Derby of the Royal Capital City of Krakow." So it's no wonder that the shorter nickname "Holy War" is used more commonly. And it fits better, too. Two weeks ago marked 100 years since this all officially started: Wisla Krakow versus MKS Cracovia, perhaps the most intense derby in the world.

When I first came to Krakow, my friends advised me to stay home on Holy War day. Not without hesitation, I went shopping and passed police in riot gear here, there and…everywhere. It's a game everyone talks about days before, but when it finally comes Krakow seems like an ocean just before the storm – abnormally silent.

It's surely not The Biggest Game in the World, as such. No chance, with stadium capacities of 6,000 and 20,000. In a few years both grounds will be rebuilt, but will still not match any of the great rivalries worldwide in terms of the scale. It won't compete with the Old Firm games in terms of frequency, either. But I doubt even the Old Firm could produce an experience comparable in terms of intensity. In fact, when I bought tickets for a few Scotsmen two years ago, they left the stadium by half-time, feeling their lives were threatened.

My club is Wisla Krakow. People call it *Biala Gwiazda* (White Star). Cracovia call us "dogs." For 40 years Wisla was owned by the communist police, and "dog" is a common term of abuse for police officers in Poland. Cracovia

35

are known as *Pasy* (Stripes) or "Jews". That's a consequence of Cracovia's supposed Jewish roots. Fans of both clubs have learned to live with these nicknames. Wisla fanatics often use the dog theme, emphasising the positive traits (bravery, loyalty, commitment), such as in the flags "Furious Dogs" or "Fidelity". Meanwhile, Cracovia's hooligans actually call themselves "Jude Gang" and their stadium's nickname is the "Holy Ground".

The stadiums are a stone's throw distance apart, just across a meadow. It looks nearly absurd when supporters are loaded into buses near one of them and escorted by armored vans to the other. They could easily walk there within five minutes. But it's not called Holy War for nothing.

BIGGER THAN WORLD WAR

The term "Holy War" was at first used to describe the rivalry of Krakow's Jewish teams, Makkabi and Jutrzenka. A defender from the latter club later joined Cracovia and during the derby game against Wisla he is supposed to have told his teammates, "Come on guys, let's win this holy war!" The phrase was then integrated into a song and became popular.

Cracovia was set to meet Wisla on September 2nd 1939. However, due to German aggression, the players were sent to battle and at least 21 never came back. When the Germans took control of Krakow, they prohibited all sporting events. Being declared by Hitler as the capital of the General Government, Krakow was the base for up to 50,000 German soldiers.

But even this didn't stop the rivalry. The "conspiracy championships of Krakow" were hosted mostly by small grounds in the outskirts of the city, but still attended by hundreds or even thousands. Needless to say, being caught during an event like this could mean death. But it was only once during the war, in 1942, that the derby did not take place. The Nazis had been informed about the time and place and so the game was abandoned when German forces started arriving.

In 1943, over 10,000 people came to cheer for their teams as the Holy War proved decisive for the Krakow conspiracy championship. When the referee gave Cracovia a penalty kick four minutes before full time, Wisla players attacked him. A moment later the whole audience was engaged in a huge fight. The battling crowd started moving and reached the district headquarters of the German SS in Podgorze. The only thing that saved people from being sent to nearby Auschwitz was the fact that the SS was governed by a former Austrian football player. When he had heard that this riot was a result of the derby game, he said: "Supporters? Then let them fight."

Just 10 days after Krakow's liberation, when the war was still going on in Europe, the city which had lost over a quarter of its population was again excited by the Holy War. The game was far from perfect – it lasted only an hour – and Cracovia's team was incomplete, whilst the referee was a Wisla fanatic (history had come full circle – the first official game in 1908 was refereed by a Cracovia player).

NOTHING WILL TEAR US APART

In the early '70s, Cracovia's position started deteriorating rapidly. Year by year they were relegated, ending up in the local league. The club was stuck there and so the Krakow derby had to take a break. But supporters couldn't stand

that thought. They convinced the authorities to celebrate the first Holy War after Krakow's liberation by hosting an annual anniversary derby.

As the games were played in late January, the timing didn't collide with the league schedule. It didn't count in the league; it was about who would be calling themselves *Pany* (Masters) for the next year.

These matches were played annually until 1990. That year brought perhaps the most unbelievable scene in Polish fan culture's history. Police officers clashed with supporters, which isn't surprising in itself. But the police intervention after the game was widely judged as far too brutal. Therefore, they were subjected to a counter-attack by Cracovia hooligans and, most surprisingly, by Wisla's fanatics as well. Side-by-side, supporters of both clubs had pushed police far into the city centre and later trashed the USSR consulate, where some of the escaping policemen had sought safety. This time the Krakow derby was prohibited for good, and no more anniversary Holy Wars have been played.

To cope with the remaining demand, the rector of Jagiellonian University organized a game in

1993. Thankfully for the rivalry, soon after that Cracovia advanced to the second division and Wisla was relegated from the top flight, so both teams could finally meet again in the league. However, Wisla soon went back up to the Ekstraklasa and so no games have been played for seven years.

In 2004, when Cracovia returned to the top flight, the first derby in the Ekstraklasa for 20 years was to be played. The game ended goalless, but for many what was happening off the pitch was more important. Over 1,600 policemen were sent to secure the game and citizens were officially asked to "avoid strolling and watch their backs when leaving home to put away the garbage."

THE DARK SIDE

The Holy War tends to have a literal meaning for some. When Wisla reserves were playing Clepardia in the Polish Cup, they had to come to a district dominated by Cracovia fans. Before the game Clepardia players supposedly told their rivals: "They'll get you after the game anyway."

Just after the final whistle, a group of up to 40 hooligans attacked the Wisla players. According to some witnesses, they were armed with knives or even axes. Before police came, several players had to run between the blocks for safety.

I've heard and read a few times that the first victim of the Holy War was the wife of a Cracovia fan in the 1930s smothered by her husband in the stadium. She was supposed to have asked him just before full time: "Which team is ours?" This might be an urban myth, but the fact is, when a couple of people approach you in the street, the last question you want to hear is "Who do you support?"

Krakow's districts are strongly divided and the map of football sympathies resembles a chessboard. One district supports Wisla, the other Cracovia, with fans of third division Hutnik being a rather outnumbered minority. If you wander around the housing estates, you'll notice various graffiti indicating whose estate it is. Those are probably the most dangerous places, rather than the stadiums: Mateusz ended up with his brain out. Filip stabbed. Kamil with an axe in his back. Michal died under baseball bats. And the list goes sadly on.

Legia fans recently refused to go to an away game in Krakow "in the name of principle." Wisla's and Cracovia's firms are the only two that haven't signed the "Poznan agreement" from a few years back, according to which firms nationwide don't use weapons in fights.

THE DERBY ITSELF

The atmosphere at the Krakow derby is hard to compare with anything. It's one of the few games when you can see the whole stands jumping. No matter if it's Cracovia's "Kto nie skacze, ten za Wisła" ("Who's not jumping is a Wisla supporter") or Wisla's jumping chants. This is where you will see a sea of hands in the air whenever the capo orders them raised. This is the game when chants are thundering onto the pitch. This is simply the game of the season, the game ultras are preparing weeks or even months before. When Cracovia returned to Ekstraklasa, "Ultra Wisla" prepared several different choreographies for one game. When Wisla celebrated their centenary in 2006, they made around 700 flags especially for that game.

And so to the final result of the 175th Holy War: on the pitch, 2-1 to Wisla, making them the *Pany*. Off the pitch, 15 seats were trashed in the away section, several enemy scarves were burnt on the fences and two minor riots with police and security came after full time (one in the home section, one in the away section). After the previous seasons, this was almost like a picnic. **pi**

US VERSUS THEM

THE SOCIAL PSYCHOLOGY OF FANDOM

ANDREW GUEST

MARCH 29ᵀᴴ 2010

WHY, WITH INTENSE and organic feelings of affiliation to our teams, does it so rarely seem to matter that the teams themselves are obviously artificial constructions? Why, in the midst of a fan revolt against an ownership group that is foreign and detached, do Manchester United fans not seem too bothered that most of their players are also 'foreign' (beyond Mancunians Gary Neville and Paul Scholes, United's 18 on Saturday included 15 non-English players)? Why, amidst the admirable growth of genuine American supporters groups, do MLS teams not seem to put much emphasis on employing local players with roots in their communities? I'd like to suggest that the emotional intensity of fan affiliation, and the fact that it persists and even grows amidst the globalization and commercialization of the game, is less about our teams and more about our minds.

I've been intrigued by the noble irrationality of fan allegiance for years, with recent events in my small corner of the soccer world further piquing my curiosity – as a current Portlander who grew up in Seattle, the MLS-fed intensification of a lingering fan rivalry has been most curious to watch. The recent tenuous claim of 'hooliganism' when a Portland fan was apparently choked with his Timbers scarf by Seattle fans after a pre-season 'friendly' was only one marker in an ongoing Pacific Northwest rivalry.

Any American reader of soccer blogs that mention the Sounders or the Timbers is certainly familiar with the phenomenon – comment threads will inevitably end up with angry references to 'S**ttle' and 'Portscum', often including exaggerated claims as to the differences between the cities. Likewise, at games themselves, chants, songs, and signs regularly transition into personal attacks that are often demonstrably irrational. I was particularly struck at a U.S. Open Cup match in Portland last year where a large double posted sign on parade in front of the sold-out crowd had a stark black and white illustration of a large rifle captioned with "KELLER - DO THE COBAIN."

Really? Suggesting Kasey Keller should commit suicide because he had at that point played 12 games for the Sounders (about one tenth as many games as he has played for the United States – of which, despite occasional efforts to declare its own people's republic, Portland is still a part)? What's more, Kasey Keller has more connections to the city of Portland than any single player on the field for the Timbers that day. Keller was an all-American at the University of Portland, and is widely credited as the key player that allowed Clive Charles to make UP a legitimate soccer power – something the city's soccer fans often note with pride. Keller even played 10 games

for a previous incarnation of the Timbers in 1989. In contrast, the Timbers starting eleven that day had exactly zero players with any childhood or college roots in Portland – and at least one player on the roster who had not even heard of Portland, Oregon, until signing a contract.

Of course the vast majority fans, even in Portland and Seattle, don't choke people with scarves or promote suicide – there are crazy people everywhere. And the edginess and intensity of passionate fan allegiance is often a crucial element of what makes a great match so much fun for everyone involved. But that doesn't make our emotional allegiance to professional teams, which are mostly artificial 'clubs' oriented to making money for rich people, any more rational.

WHAT EXPLAINS THE IRRATIONALITY OF THE SPORTS FAN?

A few weeks ago I wrote about sports psychology, and the fact that in my experience it has proven less useful for enhancing performance than explaining how the game works. So this week I'm returning to that theme and suggesting that while many factors contribute to our emotional connections to sports teams, one of the best explanations comes from social psychology.

The basic idea, drawing off social identity theory, is that for various evolutionary reasons one of our most fundamental psychological instincts is to identify and divide the world into two groups: us and them. Us is good; them is bad. In our ancestral past this instinct may have been oriented by clans, but now it is up for grabs – we are constantly, unconsciously, affiliating with cities, countries, schools, political parties, genders, ethnicities, musicians, companies, teams, and whatever else becomes salient in our daily lives. What's fascinating about this basic 'us versus them' instinct is how quickly, and irrationally, it activates. For a Portlander at a Timbers-Sounders game, Kasey Keller should rationally be one of us. But instinctively he is one of them.

There are a couple fun examples of the automaticity of 'us versus them' thinking that might be familiar to anyone who has ever taken Psychology 101. The classic is Muzafer Sherif's 1954 "Robbers Cave Experiment." Sherif was a social psychologist at the University of Oklahoma who was interested in group behavior, and devised a classic experiment elegant for its simplicity. He basically just took a group of normal boys to summer camp at Robbers Cave State Park. The trick was that the boys were randomly assigned to two separate groups and isolated from each other – adopting group names "The Rattlers" and "The Eagles" (no relation, I presume, to the Screaming Eagles "standing up for DC" United).

After an initial period of bonding, the boys learned of the other group, and the researchers began arranging for competitions on a ball field. There was almost immediate animosity; name-calling, efforts to self-segregate, raids of group camps, and, in fine supporters group tradition, the exchange of derogatory songs. The researchers added a final phase where they created situations in which the groups had to work together, and suddenly everyone started to get along again. It was a simple study making a profound point: there was no difference between the two groups of boys until they became groups. Any of the "Rattlers" could just as easily have been "Eagles" in exactly the same way as, I suspect, many Manchester United supporters could just as easily have been for Arsenal or

Liverpool with a few small twists of fate.

Another excellent example of this comes from several decades ago, when an Iowa school teacher named Jane Elliot created a brilliant demonstration of the power of "us versus them" as a way to address racial discrimination with her elementary school students in the wake of Martin Luther King Jr.'s assassination in 1968. One morning, she simply told all her students that they were going to do a little demonstration where they would be divided up for a few days by the color of their eyes.

First the blue eyed kids got the privileges, while the brown eyed kids put on colored scarves marking their out-group status (and the next day it was reversed). By recess time that same morning the kids were brawling on the playground because *us* started mocking *them* for having brown eyes. In Jane Elliot's words: "I watched what had been marvelous, cooperative, wonderful, thoughtful children turn into nasty, vicious, discriminating, little third-graders in a space of fifteen minutes." Substitute "sports fans" for "children," along with "ninety" for "fifty," and the quote still works quite well.

Further, in the classroom situation, not only did simple and substantively meaningless group distinctions based on eye color create anger, the kids let their group membership shape their performance on school work – on a flash card task the same kids either excelled or failed depending on whether their group was assigned superiority for the day. Our 'us versus them' instinct can make kids seem stupid, and I suspect it can also allow ostensibly intelligent and educated soccer fans to end up choking people with scarves.

A LABORATORY FOR GROUPNESS

It turns out that soccer and supporters groups are nearly perfect laboratories for stimulating 'us versus them' instincts. According to Judith Harris's accessible, if controversial, summary of the scholarly research, some of the key ingredients for making group membership psychologically significant include:

»Socially defined membership that necessitates more of an internal than external commitment, along with shared experiences and an emphasis on commonalities within the group

(according to the Timbers Army website, to be a member "If you like your sports passionate instead of passive – if you're proud of the Rose City – if you appreciate the Beautiful Game – YOU are Timbers Army. No membership, no initiation, no rules, no fuss. Just wander into the North End of PGE Park and join the fun!")

» Competition and an emphasis on points of contrast from other groups (when the British *European Football Weekends* website waded into explaining the Sounders versus Timbers rivalry across the pond, the comments were inundated with defensive comparisons from both sides in the Northwest: a relatively tame example from an anonymous Sounders fan, "you may wonder why Timbers fans are commenting on an article about the Sounders. They are a funny lot whose entire supporter culture revolves around jealousy of and irrevocable obsession with the Sounders. They rarely know the names of their own players, but they will mark their calendars months in advance for a match against us. If you spend time in person with a Timbers fan, you will hear more talk about the Sounders than their own team.")

» Proximity (it is no coincidence that many supporters groups mark themselves explicitly by the section of the stadium where they sit – the 107^{ist} Independent Supporters' Trust is the machinery behind the Timbers Army and is named after the stadium section where they sit during games, while the Sounders' group Emerald City Supporters have their numerical sections (121-123) and their street ("Brougham Faithful") featured on their logo.)

» Group goals and/or a common enemy (at the Sounders-Timbers match, at least one Vancouver Whitecaps supporter came to Portland bearing a sign with the message "The enemy of my enemy is my friend!").

» Explicit markers of group identity (scarves are virtually ubiquitous across the soccer world because they are such an efficient marker of group identity – one of the Sounders' marketing coups was to provide 'free' scarves to season ticket holders, automatically cementing a social identity while also bearing an eerie resemblance to the scarves Jane Elliot used to mark the "inferior" group in her classroom).

» Implicit norms and expectations (some Sounders supporters groups, such as Gorilla FC, distinguish themselves by trying to explicitly avoid the stereotypes of "ultra" groups: "One more belief of Gorilla FC, besides the love of the party, is that this group will share the same spirit as the fans of FC ST. PAULI!! WE ARE ANTI-RACIST, ANTI-FASCIST, ANTI-SEXIST, AND ANTI-HOMOPHOBIC, BUT PRO-PARTY!! It seems bizarre to have to post that, however we want to establish that our friends are dedicated to building a love of the Sounders free from ignorance. A thinking ethic! We also will be active in supporting various community organizations. Gorilla FC is more than just a supporters club!!")

As that last example makes clear, creating a sense of 'groupness' is not necessarily a bad thing – however artificial, the social identities of sports fans have just as much potential to influence pro-social as anti-social norms. In fact, the Timbers' 107[ist] Supporters Trust includes not just tifo and game travel but also charitable works among its 'basic purposes.' Likewise, when social marketing campaigns such as 'Show Racism the Red Card' work it is likely due largely to re-framing social identities – remaking the group identity to include 'soccer fans fight [rather than endorse] racism.'

But what team rivalries and fan allegiances all over the world illustrate most of all is that the 'us versus them' instinct plays fast and easy on our minds. As much as FIFA folks like to spin platitudes about the game bringing people together, it can just as easily tear people apart.

As much as the World Cup presents opportunities to display national identities, our local allegiances and teams (so often composed entirely of outsiders) display how contrived all our social identities can be. And, at the same time, how meaningful. **pi**

HISTORY

THE DARK AGES

SOCCER IN AMERICA FROM 1984 TO 1996

BENJAMIN KUMMING

FEBRUARY 13TH 2010

PROLOGUE

JULY OF 1967, in Los Angeles. A crowd of just under 18,000 looks on as the first FIFA-sanctioned, nationwide soccer championship in the United States is contested at the L.A. Memorial Coliseum. It's a historic event, in the technical sense, but in the sweep of American sporting history, the match, and its participants, have been more or less forgotten.

This is the birth of the professional game in the United States and Canada. The league, the United Soccer Association, represents the first attempt at building a truly coast-to-coast, major soccer league. And they did it with borrowed teams. On the day, the Los Angeles Wolves beat the Washington (D.C.) Whips 6-5, after extra time. The two

teams had emerged as champions of their divisions, Western and Eastern respectively, outplaying teams in 10 other major U.S. and Canadian cities.

They truly were the best in America, and yet there was nothing American about them. The entire roster of the L.A. Wolves was identical to that of Wolverhampton Wanderers from England and Washington's the same as that of Aberdeen F.C. of the Scottish First Division. To a man.

As a matter of fact, the entire league was composed of imported European and South American clubs. All of the twelve American franchises were wholesale imports, comprised of players picking up extra playing time and paychecks during the traditional summer offseason.

In addition to Wolves and Aberdeen, the others were:

» *Shamrock Rovers (Ireland):*
  Boston Rovers
» *Cagliari Calcio (Italy):*
  Chicago Mustangs
» *Stoke City (England):*
  Cleveland Stokers
» *Dundee United (Scotland):*
  Dallas Tornado
» *Glentoran F.C. (N. Ireland):*
  Detroit Cougars
» *Bangu A.C. (Brazil):*
  Houston Stars
» *C.A. Cerro (Uruguay):*
  N.Y. Skyliners
» *ADO Den Haag (Netherlands):*
  San Francisco Golden Gate Gales
» *Hibernian F.C. (Scotland):*
  Toronto City
» *Sunderland A.F.C. (England):*
  Vancouver Royal Canadians

The league only contested one season before merging with its rival National Professional Soccer League (NPSL) to form the NASL in 1968. But it certainly seems an oddly (perhaps cynically) appropriate beginning for the Great American Soccer Experiment, this importing of whole teams from European and South American leagues, considering what became of the NASL, and the Dark Ages induced by its collapse.

A 1984 *Sports Illustrated* article by Clive Gammon saw the writing on the wall as the league began what would be its last season. And yet, he must have been a lover of the game, for he closed on an optimistic, and prescient, note: "Soccer is too great a sport to be lost because of the antics of sports-illiterate owners and fast-buck seekers. Even if the NASL goes gurgling down tubes of its own making, soccer will surely come back for another life." It did, of course, in the form of the (hopefully) more stable MLS, but it was a long dark winter for the sport between 1984 and now.

AMONG THE ASHES

The collapse of the NASL didn't mean a sudden disappearance of fans or players, of course, or even many of the clubs. Most of the game moved indoors, though, and there were not a few clubs who simply vanished in the implosion. Those teams who were dedicated to the outdoor game were reduced to semi-pro status at best, while dozens of leagues sprang up across the country, changed names and then collapsed during the twelve years between the end of the NASL and the birth of MLS in 1996.

In the Pacific Northwest, for example, a handful of teams

created what was originally called the Western Alliance Challenge Series in 1985, the year after the collapse of the NASL – a sort of mini-league composed of four independent regional teams: F.C. Portland, F.C. Seattle, Victoria (British Columbia) Riptides, and what remained of the post-NASL San Jose Earthquakes.

This was the state of outdoor soccer across the country imme-diately after the NASL's demise: small regional groups of small-budget teams competing for noth-ing more than pride. Chief among them seem to have been the Lone Star Soccer Alliance in Texas, Oklahoma and Kansas (featur-ing the worst club name I came across during this research: San Antonio XLR8), the Southwest Independent Soccer League, and on the East Coast, the third league in the history of the country to call itself the American Soccer League.

These leagues were not par-ticularly stable, however, fluctuat-ing constantly in membership and name, and none of them as wildly as the Southwest Independent Soccer League. Between 1986 when it was established as an indoor league and 1997, it went through eight different names. While it was composed of

multiple divisions, over 40 of its listed member teams only existed for one season (including worst name runner-up, Ohio Xoggz). Most of those single-season teams played only in 1994, the year the United States hosted the World Cup, apparently hoping for a groundswell of interest in the club sport. Still, by the time its own dust had settled, the SISL had transformed from a small regional league into the United Systems of Independent Soccer Leagues, or USISL, and had constructed the divisional pyramid of semi-pro and developmental leagues that still operates today as the basis of lower-league soccer in the United States and Canada.

Meanwhile, the Western Soccer Challenge Series had become the Western Soccer League in 1989 and fielded teams from Arizona to Edmonton. Its opposite, the ASL, managed the miraculous: two full seasons without losing a franchise. In 1990, the two merged, form-ing the first nationwide outdoor league since the NASL: the American Professional Soccer League. Indeed, come 1994, the league would present itself to the USSF as a candidate for the Division One professional league the Federation had promised to

FIFA in exchange for hosting the World Cup. Despite being the only functioning league put forward, the APSL lost out to what would become MLS.

The league rebranded itself again, this time as the A-League, but it was in steep decline and in 1996, when most of the league's best had jumped ship to MLS, it was practically dead in the water. Enter here the ascendant USISL to absorb the A-League, which was merged with the USISL Select division.

The new joint venture retained the name A-League and operated as the 2nd Division in the U.S. and Canada for many years after, eventually being rebranded again as USL 1 – still here today, if barely. But none of these leagues could ever really lay claim to being truly *professional* in the way the NASL had been, or that MLS would become. That honor laid elsewhere, in hockey arenas.

BRINGING THE TORCH INSIDE

"Indoor soccer will be the game of the Eighties. Bet your cherries on it."
– Charley Eckman

There's a certain ironic truth to that quote, taken from a 1983 *Sports Illustrated* article on the Major Indoor Soccer League by Frank Deford. I say ironic because indoor soccer was, certainly, a sport of the Eighties, but not since. Charley Eckman was a former NCAA and NBA referee and had coached the Fort Wayne Pistons of the nascent NBA in the mid-1950s. By the mid-Eighties, though, he was the color radio commentator for the MISL's Baltimore Blast, and had become a vocal proponent of the indoor game.

And well he should have been, for the game seemed well positioned to move in on its competing indoor winter sports, hockey and basketball, neither of which had hit its peak. Consider this – searches of the *Sports Illustrated* electronic archive returned 10 articles dedicated to the MISL throughout the 1980s. Not a lot, to be sure, but a search for articles related to the predominate interim outdoor leagues discussed above returns only a suggestion to search for something else.

It's telling not only as an excuse for the sparse information presented here regarding outdoor soccer in the 1980s, but as a reading of public sentiment regarding the sport altogether.

After the collapse of the NASL, *SI* saw nothing worthy of coverage in the domestic outdoor game. When youth teams were taken on group trips to see a pro match, it was likely the MISL they saw (there may even be a St. Louis Steamers pennant lost among the collected memorabilia of my childhood somewhere). The outdoor game had failed – that was a fact. Nevermind that this was due more to poor oversight than cultural disinterest, indoor soccer was in its ascendency and no one was looking back.

In 1975, the NASL had undertaken its first-ever indoor tournament. Divided into regional groups, 16 of the 20 teams participated in the group-to-elimination competition. The San Jose Earthquakes defeated the Tampa Bay Rowdies 8 to 5. The tournament was staged again the following year, but with only 12 teams competing (the flagship New York Cosmos notably one of the abstaining teams). Tampa Bay was vindicated in the final, but the tournament was put on hiatus.

There were tentative plans to launch a full-on indoor NASL league as a supplement to the regular season, but the NASL was beaten to the punch when, in December of 1978, the Major Indoor Soccer League opened its inaugural season. Pete Rose, baseball legend and part owner of the Cincinnati Kids franchise, kicked out the first ball, and the first professional indoor soccer league in the United States was underway – six-a-side, with hockey-style boards and all. Although there were only six teams that first year, the venture was a success, and the NASL quickly followed suit, fast tracking its own plans for an indoor league that began the following winter, though many of its stars – and some entire teams – declined to participate.

The NASL-Indoor may have featured incarnations of America's top flight clubs, but it was really a doomed enterprise, formed as it was at the beginning of the end of the NASL. Teams began dropping out of the competition almost immediately, and as more and more teams folded completely, the NASL-Indoor dwindled to a paltry seven teams in the winter of '83-'84 – the last NASL competition, indoor or out, to be played. It didn't help that, during its dying days, a few teams even jumped ship to MISL. Indeed, what had been the start-up rival league grew from its original six to 14 teams in the same time span, including former NASLers like the Chicago

Sting and Minnesota Kickers and even one season of the New York Cosmos in '84-'85. Without the outdoor NASL, MISL was now the premier soccer league in the nation.

Over the next several years, attendances climbed to dizzy heights near 10,000 – more in places like St. Louis. ESPN broadcast as many as 18 games a season, and the league even had bonafide star players in Croat/ Yugoslavian Steve Zungul and the Brazilian Tatu. And, in a pattern unsurprising in retrospect, soccer-ignorant businessmen clamored for the chance to throw their millions into the show. Many a pundit (and hopeful investor) truly believed indoor soccer would be the version of the sport to capture the American market. *Sports Illustrated* writer JD Reed wrote in 1980, "Magic or human pinball, the craze may be around for a while." In many markets, the indoor teams were drawing far better crowds than their deceased and dying outdoor predecessors could.

Purists, of course, were mortified. This was not soccer, what with its hockey boards, multiple-point goal ranges, and penalty boxes. Ben Kerner, owner of the best-selling St. Louis Steamers told *Sports Illustrated's* Drank DeFord, "All right, it's not soccer. Call it something else. So what does it matter what you call it if the people enjoy it, eh? It's better than being out on the street." Former NASL goalkeeper Bob Rigby, playing in MISL in 1980 said, "Some crazy must have invented this sport. It's a zoo, a circus. I can't believe anybody takes it seriously, but they do."

Many people were stumped as to why, exactly, MISL seemed to be off to such a good start. It was, after all, a mere bastardization of a sport that was barely keeping its head above water to begin with. But it was, due in part perhaps to its own hype – which shouldn't be under-estimated.

Teams were introduced in a dazzling light show, emerging from clouds of theater fog to rousing disco tunes. Outrageous mascots (the Philadelphia Fever's eight-foot-tall, electric-light-infused Socceroo, for example) threw trinkets and toys to the crowd. The players themselves were paraded and posterized in their leg-revealing short shorts. The spectacle was most certainly Of The Eighties, and it seemed to be working.

So much so, that in 1985 MISL got a rival start-up of its

own, the American Indoor Soccer Association. The salary war that resulted saw the MISL shrink back to seven teams (only after folding and re-establishing the Tacoma Stars franchise). By 1990, a certain equilibrium between the leagues seems to have emerged, as each competed with eight teams a piece.

In 1991 both teams rebranded, becoming the Major Soccer League and National Professional League, each having dropped the "indoor" qualifier from the name – perhaps an indicator of the primacy of the indoor version of the sport at the time. But, alas – and befitting the Sport of the Eighties – it was too late. MSL collapsed the following year as attendances drooped into the 6,000s. In 1993, however, the Continental Indoor Soccer League was born, which would stage its games in summer, and would come to include Mexican teams.

Since they played on opposite schedules, the CISL and NPSL were both able to grow in the run-up to and immediately follow- ing USA '94. The CISL folded two years on, though, unable to com- pete with the summer-schedule outdoor MLS. And while the NPSL carried on for several more years – and other leagues have since come and gone – the birth of MLS was

the writing on the wall for indoor soccer. All the predictions that indoor would be the version of the sport to sweep America proved hopelessly hopeful.

Sports writers, and the pub- lic in general, have displayed an amazing ability to forget the long and complex history of associa- tion football in the United States. And yet it seems they still sting from the lessons learned from the NASL and indoor soccer, hesitant to embrace the sport that has failed them so many times before.

The future of soccer here is not guaranteed, of course, but as MLS nears its 15th season, the current top-flight organization has learned its own valuable lessons, and continues cautiously apace. It leaves one hopeful that the future will prove more steady than the past, especially since I have never heard anyone call soccer the Game of the Nineties, 2000s, or Teens. **pi**

TALES FROM THE DARK AGES
OF AMERICAN SOCCER

PETER WILT

FEBRUARY 17TH 2010

L AST WEEK BENJAMIN Kumming wrote a salient column for Pitch Invasion detailing the "Dark Ages of Soccer" in the United States. He correctly used the 1984 death of the North American Soccer League and the 1996 birth of Major League Soccer to book-end the era. It marked a dozen year period without Division One soccer in this country: the only 12 years out of the last 42 without it, in fact.

I was fortunate to be a witness to the Dark Ages from a front row seat. I guess you could even say I had a seat on the bench...and even got in the game and maybe scored a couple goals that helped return the sport to the mainstream in American soccer's mid-1990s renaissance.

As Benny points out in his piece, professional soccer was

relegated to indoor arenas and minor league outdoor venues for more than a decade, while on a parallel path, the seeds sown by the NASL on suburban parks from Miami to Tacoma were sprouting millions of youth soccer players in places that had never before seen a soccer ball.

Indoor soccer, first with the Milwaukee Wave in 1987, then with the Chicago Power in 1990, was my entry ticket to the game. In 1994, the Minnesota Thunder allowed me to go outdoors with a Division Two team in one of the country's nicest, albeit still minor league, soccer specific venues.

The sport's descent into the Dark Ages surely allowed me a lifelong career in professional sports. Without it, I would not have been accepted in soccer and would have had a difficult time advancing beyond the entry level position I maintained with the minor league Milwaukee Admirals hockey team. The existence of the indoor Milwaukee Wave – not only an indoor soccer team, but a minor league indoor soccer team – gave me the opportunity to showcase my abilities at a management level. When I was interviewed for the position of Director of Marketing and Publicity for the Wave, I confessed to not knowing anything about soccer, but knowing a lot about operations and marketing second tier sports in Milwaukee from my Admirals experience and viewing the Wave as local competition for the entertainment dollar. The team's president and co-owner told me that was exactly what he was looking for, because he was tired of "soccer people" who didn't know anything about sports business telling him what to do.

The staff member I replaced at the Wave was Dan Currier, a veteran sports PR guy who I knew. When he found out he had been replaced, but before he knew by whom, Dan called to tell me he was being let go and they were bringing in "some marketing whiz". Awkwardly, I had to admit to him that I was the culprit. It was a moment that brought me into the sport's Dark Ages and in a *deja vu* experience would similarly take me out of the Dark Ages ten years and three months later.

The dearth of sports executives with soccer experience allowed me to climb the ladder rapidly during those years. Using business strategies and tactics that I learned from Mike Wojciechowski, my boss at the Admirals, we grew our average attendance from 2,300 per game in 1987 to almost 9,000 per game when I left the Wave in December 1990 to become the Chicago Power's General Manager. Despite having sub-.500 teams each season with the Wave, our sponsorship revenue more than tripled, we signed the franchise's first television and radio agreements and our exposure in the market place led to relevancy for the first time. The methods are now commonplace, but were relatively new to professional sports at the time: saturate the community with player appearances, sell field time to youth soccer groups for games before, during and after the pro game, create attention catching promotions and use lights, fog and loud music to enhance the fan experience.

The success we enjoyed in Milwaukee gave me the

opportunity to return to my boy-hood home in 1990 as General Manager of Chicago's NPSL team. The Power had players leftover from soccer's earlier glory years like ex-Chicago Sting stars Pato Margetic, Teddy Krafft, Batata and Bret Hall. Those players, coached by Margetic, former Sting star Manny Rojas and current Chicago Fire assistant Mike Matkovich, gave me my first and in some ways most cherished champion-ship ring. We went on to win the NPSL's regular season champion-ship again the next season and achieved tremendous business growth over the next few seasons.

This was a time in American soccer when various professional indoor leagues were pulling dirty tricks à la Donald Segretti, to sabotage each other's growth in hopes of carving out larger pieces of the limited soccer pie. It was an alphabet soup of indoor leagues. The original MISL had great play-ers like Tatu, Preki, Fernando Clavijo and Steve Zungul, but it was dying. The AISA was trans-forming into the NPSL and the CISL was emerging as a sum-mer alternative. I played a small role in growing the NPSL at the expense of the over-salaried MISL via covert propaganda and infor-mation dissemination to MISL

owners and potential expansion teams in Detroit and Buffalo. It seems a bit nefarious now, but at the time it was simply promoting a better business model.

My final stop in soccer's Dark Ages was the Twin Cities as President, GM and part owner of the Minnesota Thunder. The Thunder had operated as an ama-teur team for five seasons before bringing me in to launch its professional era after the team's remarkable 1994 season when it went 18-1 in a schedule made up mainly of professional teams. The exclusively Minnesota based roster included future MLS play-ers Tony Sanneh, Manny Lagos and Amos Magee. Local stars like Gerard Lagos, Don Gramenz, John Menk, John Coughlin, John Swallen, Tim Foster, Chris Foster, Matt Holmes, Mark Abboud and Tony Peszneker had all played club or high school soccer on the same fields for years.

Coached by Thunder co-Founder and Minnesota soccer legend Buzz Lagos and enhanced by French transplant Pierre Morice, the Thunder was a true family that represented its com-munity as much or more than any soccer team this country has ever had. The ownership group was a who's who of Minnesota based business leaders such as Medtronic's Bill George, Norstan's Richard Cohen and HB Fuller's Tony Andersen.

We capitalized on the local ingredients to the team's successful recipe and marketed the Thunder as "The World's Game and Minnesota's Team." Attendance and sponsorship revenue led the USISL in 1996 when we were named the League's organization of the year. That year we also became the first American professional soccer team to travel to Japan to play J-League teams – a 2-1 loss to Shimizu S-Pulse and a 3-2 win over Gamba Osaka.

The following spring, while I was being considered for the Chicago MLS team's first general manager position, I received a phone call from John Borozzi, a Columbus Crew sales and marketing executive who I knew from his indoor days with the original MISL. Not knowing my interest in the same position, John told me that he was up for the Chicago GM job. He told me that he thought he had all the qualities and experience they were looking for, except for knowledge of the Chicago market and he was wondering if he could pick my brain, because he knew I knew Chicago well from my days with the Power.

I told John that I would be happy to answer any of his questions and give him my insights about Chicago as a soccer market, but there was something he needed to know.

As I told him about my candidacy, I could feel his heart sink and memories came flooding back from the conversation a decade earlier that ushered me into the Dark Ages of American soccer.

A month later I was introduced to the media as Chicago's first general manager amidst a sea of television lights and flash cameras at a news conference in Chicago's five-star Drake Hotel. I knew then that soccer and I had finally emerged into a bright new era for the sport. pi

RIVAL LEAGUES & PITCH INVASIONS

AMERICAN SOCCER IN 1967

TOM DUNMORE

DECEMBER 31ˢᵀ 2009

THE FAILURE OF the USL and NASL to receive sanctioning from the United States Soccer Federation (USSF) as Division Two leagues for the 2010 season, with both leagues given days to reach an interim compromise, is a reminder of the days in American soccer when the country had competing leagues fighting for FIFA and US Soccer approval.

One such year was 1966, as the success of the World Cup saw numerous rich promoters spring up to try and cash-in and establish a top-tier professional league in the United States. That year, no fewer than three well-heeled groups applied to form new FIFA-sanctioned leagues. US Soccer was at that time known as the U.S. Soccer Football Association (USSFA) and their staff of two men formed a committee to study the proposals, announcing they would only approve one league.

The popularity of the 1966 World Cup, televised on NBC, and the apparent riches around the corner seen by the promoters of each group, made a merger of all three groups to form one league impossible to pull off. And meanwhile, also smelling the gravy train, the USSFA suddenly upped their affiliation fee substantially: from $25 for a league to $25,000 per club.

Eventually, two competing leagues emerged: two of the groups merged to form the National Professional Soccer League (NPSL). The NPSL baulked at paying the USSFA's fees (instead attempting to negotiate directly with FIFA). Meanwhile, the third group – initially known as the North American Soccer

League – renamed itself the United Soccer Association (USA) to avoid confusion with the NPSL and agreed to pay the USSFA's substantial fees. The USA thus became, in late 1966, the only FIFA-sanctioned division one league in the United States.

Meanwhile, the NPSL decided to play anyway as an outlaw league, announcing it would begin games as early as spring 1967 and that it had a substantial national network television contract with CBS, a purported $1 million annual deal.

Neither league was short of money. Steve Holroyd describes what happened next, as the two leagues rushed to beat each other to the punch.

"The USA believed that it could not construct its own teams from scratch in nine months, yet it did not want to let the NPSL have the public's attention to itself in 1967. As a result, it decided to import foreign teams (à la the ISL) to represent its franchises, with its own teams being constructed for the following year. Twelve cities were organized for the beginning of June 1967. Meanwhile, the NPSL announced it would start two months earlier, with 10 clubs all pieced together in a few months by signing itinerant players from virtually every country around the globe.

"Desperately pursuing a market neither league could be sure existed, the opening season became a wild spending spree, with a few annual budgets approaching $1 million. When the dust settled, two leagues would be playing professional soccer in 1967, dividing a market that heretofore had showed only limited evidence of being able to support one. Alas, yet another American soccer precedent had been set: common sense would play a small role in the governing of the sport."

Neither league was a success in 1967, with overpaid administrators and chaotic organization. The USA league's commissioner, a former Major League Baseball executive called Dick Walsh, even admitted "I don't know the difference between a soccer ball and a billiard ball."

The NPSL, meanwhile, had little hope of attracting any of the world's leading players as they faced FIFA sanction for playing in an outlaw league. A bizarre collection of international players were recruited, most understandably at the end of their careers and coming for one last pay day – Chicago signed former West German international Horst Szymaniak, for example, long past his best. The Los Angeles Toros featured players speaking twelve different languages, coached by Max Wozniak from Poland, and held English classes for the squad.

In particularly short supply were American players, though Willy Roy – who had moved to the States from Germany as a small boy – would win Rookie of the Year after scoring 17 goals in 27 games for the Chicago Spurs.

The USA league, however, had no Americans at all, as in order to field any kind of a league to compete with the NASL, they simply imported foreign teams wholesale for a summer season: Ireland's Shamrock Rovers became the Boston Rovers, Italy's Cagliari suited up as the Chicago Mustangs, and so on. Wolverhampton Wanderers were at least recognisable as the Los Angeles Wolves, given "film star treatment", as Wolves player Derek Dougan later put it.

Teams in the NPSL and the USA league rented out huge venues, with the New York teams in both leagues playing at Yankee Stadium. The Wolves played the Houston Stars in the space-age Houston Astrodome in their season opener, reportedly the world's first ever soccer game on artificial turf, in front of an impressive crowd of 34,965.

CBS' broadcasts of the NPSL faced that age-old problem for American television: the need to fit in commercial breaks. Embarrassingly for all involved, injuries and fouls were concocted and lengthened to fill the need for breaks in play.

The debut of the NPSL on CBS received a mixed reaction. 8,434 watched the hometown Baltimore Bays beat the Atlanta Chiefs, with Danny Blanchflower providing the color commentary. *Sports Illustrated* reported that the game was a qualified success:

"Overall, judging by the Baltimore-Atlanta TV presentation, soccer has much to offer and, potentially, a large audience. It has the advantage, even with this not quite top-grade class of performance, of continuous motion, exciting and sometimes violent action and obvious rules easy to understand. It is rather like hockey on a grand scale, but with a ball easy enough to see that the goal-scoring is never lost to view

"The class of play in the nontelevised league is likely to be better than that in the National Professional Soccer League, since the United Soccer Association, with the blessing of the FIFA, imports entire teams to represent its cities, rather than a melange of over or under-age players. Not too long from now the two leagues are expected to merge. When they do, and when the brand of soccer offered the American public on the field and on television begins to approach the caliber of the soccer played in Europe and South America, then the game in the U.S. may become a real threat to baseball, with which it presently competes.

"Opening day in Philadelphia saw 14,163 people on hand (admittedly many of them American hyphenates) as the Spartans beat Toronto 2-0. The same day the baseball Phillies drew only 9,213 and the 76ers 9,426.

SI concluded hopefully that "The advent of soccer in the U.S. was a bit shaky. But with a Danny Blanchflower to lend spice to the TV broadcasts, a bit more intelligent presentation of the stars on the teams and a leavening of local talent, the game may yet develop into an attraction."

Crowds quickly collapsed in both leagues, though, reaching as low as 870 for a Chicago Spurs game against the Los Angeles Toros in June at Soldier Field. The USA league fared little better, with few more attending the Chicago Mustangs games at Comiskey Park

This did not mean there was no passionate play to be found, especially given the abysmal standard of refereeing and fierce competition. A Detroit Cougars match against the Houston Stars became a free-for-all: fans invaded the pitch, the players fought using corner flags as weapons and the match was abandoned. Cougars player-coach John Colrain was later suspended for punching a linesman.

Similarly, a match in New York saw fans chasing the referee around the field: as the *Times* put it, "Fleeing for his life, like some rabbit caught in the headlights of a car, the referee stumbled and fell at first base on the baseball diamond." Another pitch invasion in Toronto just days later saw the game abandoned.

The USA league ended the season with a 7,890 average attendance, with Wolves crowned as champions in July, after a classic final in which they beat the Washington Whips 6-5 in overtime in front of 17,824 fans. The NPSL finished in October, average crowds having dwindled to under 5,000, with the Oakland Clippers beating the Baltimore Bays 4-2 in a two-legged final.

It was obvious to all that the two leagues would not survive on their own; many clubs had lost over half a million dollars in one summer.

A further incentive for the USA league to bring the NPSL into its FIFA-sanctioned fold was surely the $18 million antitrust suit the NPSL had filed against the USA league, the USSFA and FIFA. The official parties agreed to an amnesty for the players who had taken part in the outlaw NPSL, the lawsuit was dropped, and the two leagues decided to merge in December 1967. And so the North American Soccer League was born. pi

THE JOB THAT WASN'T

SIR BOBBY ROBSON'S FIRST MANAGERIAL

APPOINTMENT WITH THE VANCOUVER ROYALS

RICHARD WHITTALL

FEBRUARY 17ᵀᴴ 2010

IT SEEMED NOTHING more than a routine friendly, remarkable only perhaps for providing the first proper international meeting between Canada and England in the modern era (earlier encounters were played between representative sides). And while the result was closer than most bookies had predicted – a 1-0 win for England with Mark Hateley's goal from a Glenn Hoddle free kick in the 59th minute saving face for Sir Bobby Robson's team—the warm-up match for the World Cup in Mexico played on May 24th 1986 at Swangard Stadium BC would have been routine to just about everyone. Everyone, save perhaps Sir Bobby Robson.

While he made no comment on the subject, one cannot help think Robson had some idea of the significance of his visit to Canada prior to his first major international tournament as England boss. It was, after all, British Columbia that gave the former Fulham star his very first managerial position – appointed by the Vancouver Royals of the United Soccer Association (USA) in May 1967.

The legendary manager's first appointment was not a success. In fact it wasn't much of anything. The year leading up to the birth of the North American Soccer League (NASL) was a tumultuous one, with two newly formed North American soccer leagues, the USA and the National Professional Soccer League (NPSL), locked in a death grip for supporters, television rights and FIFA-sanctioned legitimacy.

Neither league provided a sustainable model for growing

the game in America. The USA was comprised in its first season entirely by proxy sides from Europe and South America – the Royals were in fact Sunderland on summer holidays – while the NPSL's status as an unapproved FIFA 'outlaw' forced it to recruit from the professional dregs, severely curtailing the quality of play. A merger was a practical inevitability, and as with all mergers there were layoffs.

Robson had been hired presumably to manage the Royals after the USA's inaugural 'proxy' season, but things changed when the USA and NPSL merged to form the NASL. The USA's San Francisco Golden Gate Gales joined the Vancouver Royals in BC. The Gales' player-manager at the time was Ferenc Puskas, whose name alone was enough to oust Robson from the top job with Vancouver. According to the excellent Sunderland fansite rokerpark.com, Sir Bobby was offered an assistant managerial position. He refused. It would be the first of several early managerial missteps.

An article from the *Toronto Daily Star* in November 1968 gleefully tracks Robson's subsequent failings. Hired in January 1968 to manage Fulham, he bungled an attempt to sell injured Fulham and England legend Johnny Haynes to the New York Generals for $10,000. Wrangling over Haynes' injury dragged on until the Generals disappeared altogether with the birth of the NASL. Fulham were relegated that May from League One, and while Robson escaped blame for the drop, he couldn't evade the wrath of Fulham's board members as the club slipped down the League Two roster early in the 1968-69 season. He was sacked eight months into a three-year appointment. Bitterest of all for Robson must have been Fulham's subsequent decision to appoint Haynes as player-manager.

Robson had, of course, the strength of mind to go on to a successful thirteen-year stint with Ipswich, and then in 1982 to the England job. While it's impossible to know if his return to British Columbia in charge of one of the world's most storied sides felt something like vindication for Sir Bobby, his customary charm didn't show it. As the *Toronto Star* (May 25, 1986) noted after the Canada friendly, "Bobby Robson had more praise for the Canadians than he did for his own team," singling out keeper Paul Dolan and centre half Randy Samuel for their stalwart defending. His vote of confidence for the Canadian defenders

certainly must have been a boost a
week before Canada's first group
match against France, which
Canada lost by a dignified score
of 1-0. In any case his words
lacked any hint of bitterness, an
important gesture from a smiling
conqueror finally returning to the
far-off and inauspicious birthplace
of his legendary career. **pi**

THE CURRENTS OF HISTORY

WHAT DOES IT TAKE TO WIN THE WORLD CUP?

SUPRIYA NAIR

JULY 5ᵀᴴ 2010

"WHAT DOES IT take to win the World Cup?" asked Henry D Fetter of *The Atlantic* a couple of days ago, in a post called "What It Takes To Win The World Cup."

"Past results suggest that going through a period of dictatorial government is almost a *sine qua non* for a nation to be a champion."

Brian at *The Run of Play* did a very good job crushing that idea. "… [C]orrelation doesn't imply causation; the fact that two things occurred simultaneously doesn't prove that one caused the other without a mechanism to demonstrate the cause. Fetter gestures toward such a mechanism – "soccer prowess proved a national morale builder for the dictatorships of the last century" – but while it holds up in some specific cases (Mussolini, *et. al.*),

as a general theory it's just silly, especially considering that, as Fetter himself points out, most of the World Cup-winning countries that have had dictators since 1930 weren't actually dictatorships at the time when they lifted the trophy."

The idea memed, nonetheless. (I'm shocked that highbrow soccer dorks – my favourite phrase this World Cup, used by *The New Republic's* Goal Post to describe their ideal reader base – appear *not* to check RoP before coffee.) Laughable, snobbish solipsism – it's not just for FIFA anymore, kids. The soccer blogosphere has no shortage of writers doing sterling work dissecting the politics of the World Cup and men's football in thoughtful, moving ways (occasional Pitch Invasion writer Jennifer Doyle, of From a

Left Wing, is just one of them). But who needs all that when the USA's finest journalists are sitting around a table writing football stories that are the intellectual equivalent of those Hitchens-Amis word games where they mad-libbed book titles with 'sex' and 'prick'?

Last week, the phenomenon's most high-profile instance was a piece by Roger Cohen in the *New York Times* called 'Özil the German', an op-ed ostensibly exploring the multiculturalism of Germany, and the shattering of its team's power structure with the absence of 'Big Man' Michael Ballack.

"Perhaps it's not a bad thing that the first African World Cup has seen stars fail where they were not backed by teamwork. Cameroon, with its Big Man Samuel Eto'o of Inter Milan, and Ivory Coast, with Big Man Didier Drogba of Chelsea, are both out. Ghana, meanwhile, has endured through discipline and coordination.

"Africa needs more of that kind of spirit."

Ignoring the warning bells that usually ring in my head when the word 'Africa' appears in a newspaper that takes ads from the Government of Sudan and has in the past reported extensively on the Congo civil war without once mentioning its international backers, I read on.

"Since decolonization began in the second half of the 20th century, it has too often been the continent of "The Big Man." That was the sobriquet V.S. Naipaul gave in "A Bend in the River" to the African dictator plundering the city of Kisangani in Congo through mercenaries granted license to run amok.

"The colonizer's plundering merely gave way to the Big Man's impunity in stripping Africa's assets bare."

Many things about African football became clearer at once to me. Unlike the rest of the world, African football runs on the transitive properties of morality. Losing because of bad tactics and positioning, like Cameroon, conceals the deeper flaw of playing their best player – an inspirational, talented, eloquent man with almost all the qualities of a great leader – *at all*. How dare manager Paul Le Guen attempt to shoulder the blame for setting Eto'o adrift in a formation where his coordination with Webo failed repeatedly and his ability to track back was severely limited by his having to run between left and centre? The blame is Africa's for producing a player who is celebrated back home as much as he is in white cities like Barcelona and Milan. Memories of the Barnes Theory Of Socialist Righteousness pierce the heart.

As for Côte d'Ivoire, it's all very well for white people to give a man credit for stopping a civil war in his country. But ask him to play with a broken arm in order to bolster a team in a challenging group and reap the whirlwind, CIV. Given the paucity of Big Men in the rest of the group – no seriously, Kaka? Ronaldo? No civil wars! No Big Manhood! Oh, and Jong Tae-se who? – this was just as indicative of 'African tragedy' as any history of dictators in the Congo. Mobutu Sese Seko, your football Nazgul have failed you. Africa won and you lost.

Cohen is merely patting his column into shape at this point. The blissfully oblivious *New York Times* enjoys supporting the idea that the post-colonial world is self-sufficient and self-determining to such an extent that the origins of the 'Big Man' phenomenon in the support of African extremists by their former colonisers doesn't seem to merit the status of rumour, much less truth, in their pages. Rest easy, readers;

coltan wars, oil genocides and repeatedly invalidated democratic elections happen because Africans are just reverting to type. On the other hand, Cohen points out,

"[South Africa] has resisted the devastating "Big Man" syndrome. Over the past 16 years, South Africa has had four free elections and four presidents...[a] robust judiciary and free press... [t]he interaction, under the law, of various interest groups...This is its great lesson for a continent where, by 2025, one in four of every person under 24 will live."

From which statement we can infer the following:

» All African countries have the same history.
» All African countries have the same set of problems.
» Big Men are okay with us if they are Big Men by Committee, which is to say that they are Big Men who can be safely invited to speak at G20 gatherings.
» It's fine that he brokered the most incredible nation-building negotiation in the last fifty years and possibly ever, but what would really symbolise a betrayal of big man Mandela's anti-Big Man policies, more than Zuma and the ANC's drift away from his vision, would be if Siphiwe Tshabalala were

a thirty-a-season goalscorer for Manchester United.

At this point Roger Cohen is satisfied with the lesson he has just taught his African readers, and returns to the subject of multicultural Germany and the meaning of Mesut Özil.

"A Social Democrat once told me that the country's ultimate victory over Hitler would lie in the reconstitution of the Jewish community, then being pursued by luring Jews of the former Soviet Union. I always thought that was a vain, slightly kitschy idea."

Parsing issues aside, since vanity and kitschiness are things that Hannah Arendt, the great analyst of European totalitarianism, would have resisted in her political philosophy, this seems sound. Reconciliation and reparation, as Arendt knew, are overwhelmingly difficult, and sometimes even tragic ideas. (*Guernica* magazine recently posted a horrifying exploration of how, in the context of some African history, they can simply be another form of torture.)

They can be begun by legislation, but history's best hope is only ever that such acts may go on to form a new chapter. They cannot erase or change the one that has already been made. That is indeed the cause and effect of kitsch and vanity.

But the Germany of Özil and Aogo is such a victory over the Big Man who destroyed Europe.

Which is to say: thank you Turkey and Nigeria for bearing the brunt of the history of European imperialism in your own distinct ways. Directly or indirectly, we dismantled your countries in our world wars, plundered your resources, broke up your nations, sold off the pieces, put your worst enemies in power over you, treated your people like shit when they came to Europe looking for work, and continue to do so. But our football teams are now full of brown kids and black kids. So Hitler lost and you lost, but we all won. So we're cool, right? We're cool.

Roger Cohen says:

"Africa, take note"

Thank *you* for taking note, *New York Times*, and other 'highbrow' American soccer writers. We know now that you see the currents of history where the rest of us are trying – sometimes for painful reasons of our own – to see football games. But please remember that if other people wore the same smug-coloured glasses as you, your theories would undergo a fundamental shift. Where you see

models of correlation/causation
between dictators and football
victories, others would see the
run of play as the rest of the world
knows it: of a history of possession dominated by those who
wrote the rules, of enforced migra-
tions and unwilling recruitments,
of fallouts of totalitarianism
where there is no such thing as an
'almost *sine qua non*'; of contests
that we must always resist seeing
as wars, because they can only
ever be only fought – and won –
on the field. **pi**

FOOTBALL IN COLONIAL AFRICA

JACK LORD

FEBRUARY 1ˢᵀ 2008

THE COMMON IMAGE of African football is of a dusty field, a rag ball, rickety wooden goalposts, and a bunch of shoeless kids playing for fun. There is an element of truth to this cliché because Africa's uneven poverty does not facilitate great equipment and, as in the rest of the world, people are prepared to improvise to get a game going. But the early history of the game suggests that African football is more complex and sophisticated. It is a history of money, racism, tactics and magic. In Africa, in fact, the story of football is not just a game: encoded within it is all the complexity of Africa's colonial experience.

ORIGINS

Like many other colonial imports, football was a European invention, but one popularized through the grassroots enthusiasm and organization of Africans. Some missionaries promoted the game because they believed it would instil the values of sobriety, obedience, selflessness and cooperation. Other teams were founded to satisfy the demand from Africans who had seen, and imitated, Europeans playing the game. In any case, Africans soon gained effective control of these teams or, after chafing against European interference, set up independent alternatives.

Teams were followed by local football associations. South African towns had associations by the 1910s, other colonies developed them later. These associations administered various competitions, paid dues to the municipal authorities for their services, and hired bands to entertain matchday crowds. Their rise was linked to another colonial import, literacy, because associations had to arrange matches and arbitrate disputes in writing, and file their accounts with the government.

As this level of organization suggests, Africans did not simply take to football for the sheer joy of the game. There were also more hard-nosed reasons for football's success. Football was rapidly monetised and provided a useful supplementary income for players. Teams negotiated hard over appearance fees, transport allowances and prize money. In friendly matches it was common for the winning side to take sixty per cent of the prize fund, and the losers forty per cent.

This commercialization was often frowned upon by Europeans. In the late-1930s, a missionary in Northern Rhodesia complained that "all the star teams play for money." The same missionary also witnessed a match in which the visitors bet on themselves to win and confidently spent their stake in the local beer hall: "unfortunately they lost and the match ended in a free fight in which spectators joined." In urban areas, football clubs were often combined with mutual aid societies and played a valuable social role.

Migrant workers, for example, used football clubs to replace the material and social support they had left behind in their rural homes.

The style of football played in colonial Africa shifted with fashion, experience and external influence. There is a common belief that Africans excelled at stylish, attacking football, and relied on ostentatious displays of individual skill. There is some truth to this, but there was a definite tension between this kind of showy, individualistic football, and the discipline and teamwork of a winning formula.

Africans were not completely isolated from wider trends in football, and were quick to adopt new techniques and strategies. Tours of South Africa by Motherwell in the 1930s were a popular sensation, and their tight passing game and collective ethos inspired a tactical revolution among local teams.

In 1950s Brazzaville, a French coach rebelled against the prevailing British style in place and his team dominated the league with short passes and man-marking. And an upstart team in Ghana during World War Two promised more vaguely that its 'tactics' would defeat the 'dribbling' of their rivals. African football was itself a symbol of modernity, and Africans strove to keep the game up to date – but there was a distinctly African twist to it.

WITCHDOCTORS

The organizers of Ghana 2008 are keen to project the modernity of African football: sponsorship by a booming mobile phone network; the multinational advertising billboards; and the interior shots of gleaming stadia as the players wait for kick-off. But there is nonetheless a historical truth behind older media sensationalism about chicken sacrifice and witchdoctors in African international football. The game was rapidly assimilated into local religious practices, and the practical business of winning matches is often given a supernatural boost. Talismans, prayers and medicines were a valid – and expensive – part of match preparations. Team names like the Cape Coast Mighty Dwarves reflected aspects of local mythology. In Northern Rhodesia, dead ancestors continued to influence the world of the living, and football skills apparently transferred into the afterlife.

One Copperbelt team was reported in the 1950s to be making midnight pleas at the grave of a famous player: "Pump this football for us we beg you and make it light for our goalkeeper and heavy for theirs." The resort to spiritual tactics appalled some Europeans. Missionaries were especially keen to promote their more saintly teams, but the popularity of the game forced them to compromise with local beliefs. Priests in Congo-Brazzaville were outraged at the decision of a Catholic mission team to intimidate its opponents by renaming itself The Black Devils, and agreed to the name change only after players and fans began to boycott mass.

RACISM

This outline of the early history of football in Africa is perhaps too positive. The game had a darker side: football reflected both the injustices of colonialism, and the internal divisions of African societies. Football in Africa first reflected the fundamental racial divide of colonialism. In settler societies like South Africa, teams and associations were strictly segregated on colour lines. And because football was a popular childhood game, it exposed Africans to inequality from an early age. It was a revelation for Ahmed Ben Bella, the first president of independent Algeria, that his new school had two football teams: one French, one Arab. But it is also true that football transcended some racial barriers, if only temporarily and for small numbers of people. In Northern Rhodesia, for example, white spectators were a common presence at African matches.

But the barrier between black and white was not the only division in African societies, or in African football. Teams often reflected identities based on religion and class. In Obuasi, Ghana, Muslims played in a separate Mahommedans team. In Congo Brazzaville, there were separate football teams for the clerks and manual workers of colonial enterprises. And football also reflected growing ethnic rivalries within multi-ethnic states.

For example, in 1942 the New Britons, a team from Tarkwa in southwestern Ghana, resolved at their AGM "to crush down in this year all the Kotoko Teams." Kotoko, a common team name, meant porcupine and was also a symbol of Asante nationhood. The club motto of Asante Kotoko was "Thousand Killed, Thousand Comes." This referred to the

military strength of the defeated Asante Empire, now a constituent part of Britain's Gold Coast colony. But the motto was also a measure of Asante's political tenacity and was later associated with the National Liberation Movement – an Asante rival to the multi-ethnic nationalist party that led Ghana to independence. By September 1942, the Mighty Britons had defeated four Kotokos, scoring 14 goals and conceding just four. Football, then, was a very public and ritualised expression of divided African loyalties: and such divisions would play a significant role in Africa's post-colonial instability.

COLONIAL SOCIETY

African football was also affected by the structural inequalities of colonial society, and African football associations encountered the same constraints as non-sporting organizations. Europeans were suspicious of activities and organizations they did not control, and often sought to restrict their activities or co-opt their leadership. Missionaries were hostile to the perceived immorality of players and boisterous fans in independent teams. And efforts by Africans to retain and extend their footballing autonomy were ultimately limited by their political and economic weakness. Teams often relied on grants for equipment and uniforms. Stadia and playing fields were normally owned by the municipal authorities – and these were under European control.

African footballers and organizers thus had limited leeway to promote their own interests. One Ghanaian team from a mining town complained that it was impossible to fulfil their fixtures on days when the mines team played, and poached their players. And in Congo-Brazzaville, Catholic missionaries took so much of the gate receipts that the players lamented that they "did not even have lemonade money." The lack of political power also precluded wider pan-African organisation. The first international club championship in 1950, between teams from Belgian Congo and South Africa, was organised by European officials to generate favourable propaganda for colonialism.

Football was also used to achieve and display social status in competitive colonial society. This could be the prestige of personal skill, as for the Ghanaian Ekow Glenland, who told the FA he was "commonly known as Kimpo the Devil Boy." Zulu players were given praise-names previously reserved for warriors and chiefs. Other nicknames were drawn from the movies (Fu Manchu) or consumer culture (Buick), and demonstrate the extent to which colonial social status had become inseparable from symbols of western affluence. Football also bestowed prestige by association. The patron of Asante Kotoko was none other than Agyeman Prempeh II – Prempeh was the Asantehene (the Asante king), an office abolished then later reinstated by the British. A financial patron of a football team could also transfer his loyalties into local political support, and often interfered in tactical matters.

The early history of African football is complex and fascinating, and much of the story has yet to be uncovered. But the more historians discover, the more certain it becomes that in colonial Africa, football was never just a game. pi

YDNEKATCHEW TESSEMA

FORGOTTEN HERO OF AFRICAN SOCCER

TOM DUNMORE

JULY 15TH 2010

NATIONAL TEAM PLAYER, national team coach for his country's only major international triumph, co-founder of his continent's FIFA confederation, president of that confederation for 15 years, and in many ways the man who set in motion the whole chain of events that led to South Africa becoming the first African nation to host the World Cup: the late Ethiopian visionary Ydnekatchew Tessema deserves greater prominence in the annals of soccer history than he has received.

Tessema's remarkable story intertwined with decolonisation, the fight against apartheid in South Africa and the battle for respect and opportunities for African soccer in the face of a Eurocentric FIFA.

Tessema, born in 1921, was a hell of a player (scorer of 318 goals in 365 games for Saint-George SA) and a coach: in the latter role, he took his native Ethiopia to their sole major tournament triumph at the 1962 Africa Cup of Nations.

But it was as an administrator that Tessema left his true imprint on the sport. In 1953, four African nations attended the FIFA Congress for the first time: Egypt, Ethiopia, South Africa and Sudan. At first, FIFA resisted African claims for representation on its Executive Committee; in *The Ball Is Round*, David Goldblatt says "Initially their efforts had been brusquely rebuffed by FIFA's European majority on the grounds of a barely disguised and contemptuous racism."

The African nations, though, found support from the Soviet bloc and South America, and thcy gained representation on the Executive Committee in 1954 (Engineer Abdelaziz Abdallah Salem of Egypt became the first African to sit on it) and earned the right to set up their own FIFA Confederation.

That confederation, the *Confédération Africaine de Football* (CAF), was formed at a Constitutional Assembly on 8 February 1957. Tessema (still a player in his mid-thirties) was one of the delegates there representing the four countries present: Egypt, Ethiopia, Sudan and South Africa. The Statutes of CAF were drawn from those proposed by Tessema and Sudan's Abdel Rahim Shaddad. Tessema was voted onto the body's first executive committee, with Engineer Salem the first president.

Immediately, CAF faced a major crisis, with founding member South Africa under its Apartheid regime stating it could only take either an all-white or all-black team to the first Africa Cup of Nations to be held that year; CAF excluded them from the competition and threw South Africa out of CAF altogether in 1961. It was, according to fellow founding CAF delegate Abdel Halim Mohammed, Tessema's "firm stand" at CAF meetings that South Africa must field a mixed team which had ensured the confederation was the first international organisation to isolate South Africa in the sporting world. In 1963, Tessema became the Vice-President of CAF, and then led the move to form Africa's first continental club competition, the African Cup for Champion Clubs. In 1966, Tessema (fluent in French, English and Spanish) joined FIFA's Executive Committee, at a critical moment for African football in FIFA's halls of power. As CAF's membership rapidly grew, so would – theoretically – its voting power in the FIFA Congress. FIFA operated under (and still does) a one member, one vote policy at the FIFA Congress: meaning that for every African country taken in, the power of its original European members was weakened. Sir Stanley Rous, head of FIFA, stated bluntly the fears this brought up for the existing powerbase:

"Many people are convinced that it is unrealistic, for example, that a country like England, where the game started and was first organised, or that experienced countries like Italy and France, who have been pillars of FIFA and influential in its problems and in world football affairs for so many years, should have no more than equal voting rights with any of the newly created countries of Africa and Asia."

Writing in the 1980s as that sentiment lingered on, Tessema had an eloquent response to such patriarchal perspectives still permeating the international game:

"Although we acknowledge the role played by certain continents in the creation of FIFA, its development and their moral, material and financial contributions, we estimate that democratic rule dictates that all rights and duties that form an international organisation should be the same for all. This is why in the framework of legitimacy, and by following a process consistent with the interests of world football and its unity, a progressive equilibrium of representation in the heart of FIFA and its competition is required."

CAF's rise in the 1960s, meanwhile, was tightly linked to the wave of pan-Africanism sweeping the continent. National pride became linked to joining the African community of football in membership of CAF. Politics and football were seen as reflections of each other.

This led to an almighty fight between CAF and FIFA over both politics and football as African demands for more power within FIFA's governance structure reflected the demands of decolonisation politically in the international arena. Tessema's fight against racial discrimination in the African continent became a part of this struggle.

It was at this time that CAF fought its battle with FIFA to gain an automatic place for Africa at the World Cup finals. CAF had 30 members by the mid-1960s, but only half a place at the World Cup finals: the winner of the Africa Cup of Nations faced a playoff against the Asian Cup winner to qualify. The costs of competing and the low likelihood of qualification for the World Cup meant many poorer countries did not enter CAF's premier competition. And this in turn, in a clever sleight of hand by FIFA's existing European and South American powerbase, threatened their use of their growing membership in FIFA's sovereign Congress: FIFA decreed that "National Associations which do not take part in two successive World Cups or Olympic tournaments will be stripped of their right to vote at the Congress until they fulfil their obligations in this respect."

Tessema and CAF's leadership, with the global voice of

Ghana's first post-independence leader Kwame Nkrumah supporting them, announced a boycott of the 1966 World Cup unless Africa received one full place at future finals. FIFA's response was to fine the threadbare boycotting nations 5,000 Swiss Francs each. Tessema wrote a furious letter to FIFA pointing out the absurdity that only one World Cup place was awarded to a total of 65 nations in the continents outside Europe and South America. FIFA relented, and Africa was awarded a full place for the 1970 World Cup finals (Morocco becoming the first African nation to play in the World Cup since Egypt in 1934). This was to the dismay of Brain Glanville (still a *World Soccer* columnist today), who wrote that "It is quite true that football in countries such as the U.S.A. and Ethiopia would be encouraged by World Cup participation, but only at the expense of cheapening the World Cup, a pretty heavy price to pay when this tournament is, or should be, the very zenith of the International game."

Not coincidentally, politics as well as World Cup positions were dividing CAF and FIFA: led by Sir Stanley Rous, FIFA secretly supported the establishment of a new, second Confederation in Africa, the Southern African Confederation, a South African puppet clearly aimed at giving the Apartheid regime legitimacy, as South Africa had been suspended from FIFA against Rous' wishes in 1961 under pressure from CAF (FIFA's Executive Committee had lifted the suspension in 1963 following a visit by Rous to South Africa, only for the FIFA Congress to reimpose it the next year). Led by Tessema, CAF's delegation threatened to walk out on the FIFA Congress in London in 1966 if FIFA's leadership backed the reinstatement of South Africa again.

Meanwhile, internally in CAF, Tessema continued to modernise the organisation and expand its role in Africa, even as he faced challenges in a power struggle for CAF leadership. He led a key Organising Committee that resulted in a restructuring of CAF in 1972, and the same year was elected as its president (a position he would hold until his death in 1987). The continent's first youth competition was soon instituted, as was an African Cup Winners' Cup tournament. CAF's revenue grew, with television and marketing rights to the Africa Cup of Nations profitably sold for the first time in 1982, and it became less reliant on outside support and focused on continental development of the game.

Tessema had worked hard to grow Africa's standing globally, particularly in the face of intransigent European leadership at FIFA. One key strategy he employed was to cement ties between the African continent and South America, with an African select team appearing at the 1972 Brazilian Independence Cup, for example. Tessema then played a key role in the victory of Brazilian João Havelange over the reactionary Sir Stanley Rous for the FIFA presidency in 1974: for all his later corrupt dealings, that victory by Havelange was crucial for orientating FIFA beyond its previous Northern European pole and led to unprecedented opportunities for African teams.

Notably, rather than Havelange manipulating CAF to gain their support to defeat Rous, it was Tessema who had used the leverage of the forthcoming 1974 election to force Havelange to withdraw Brazil from a 1973 multi-sports festival in South Africa aimed at giving the Apartheid regime international credibility. As Rous himself wrote: "The Brazilians withdrew, I am told on good authority, because

Tessema, the president of the African confederation threatened that Mr Havelange would lose the support of the African associations in his fight against me for the presidency of FIFA."

Paul Darby, in his excellent book *Africa, Football, and FIFA: Politics, Colonialism, and Resistance*, explains Tessema's sophisticated strategy:

"The fact that Tessema was in a position to threaten the withdrawal of African support for Havelange's presidential challenge illustrates that CAF was not only gaining confidence to assert itself within world football politics but was also beginning to recognise the potential that its voting powers offered the African continent. Indeed, it is clear from African accounts of the 1974 FIFA Congress…that the African nations did not see themselves merely as pawns in a power struggle for the control of FIFA. Instead, they saw Havelange as the means through which to achieve a realignment of the distribution of power and privilege within world football which would more adequately reflect their growing stature."

At the same FIFA Congress, a motion by Tessema required the automatic expulsion from FIFA of any country that practiced "ethnic, racial and/or religious discrimination in its territory," thus ending – to the chagrin of Rous – the ambiguity that surrounded South Africa: Rous was still pushing to end their suspension. But Havelange's victory ended that hope, and under his leadership, South Africa were expelled from FIFA in 1976.

In 1978, the number of World Cup places Africa should hold came up again at FIFA, but this time, it was an easier fight for Tessema to win some numerical justice for Africa: their number of places doubled at the 1982 World Cup in Spain to two.

As the years went on, some began to question Tessema's long tenure, and the divisions between African nations hampered the realisation of the Pan-African dreams of the 1960s. But Tessema remained a force for the good of the sport until his death in 1987: he was a lone voice advocating to keep alcohol and tobacco sponsorship out of African football, and he warned against the growing trend of young African talent leaving for European shores. He spelled out the latter concern clearly in the 1980s:

"African football must make a choice! Either we keep our players in Africa with the will power of reaching one day the top of the international competitions and restore to African people a dignity that they long for; or we let our best elements leave their countries, thus remaining the eternal suppliers of raw material to the premium countries, and renounce, in this way, to any ambition. When the rich countries take away from us, also by naturalisation, our best elements, we should not expect any chivalrous behaviour on their part to help African football."

One wonders what Tessema would make of African football today: a World Cup host, with numerous world stars, but still struggling for domestic development in the game.

Shortly before his death, Tessema, according to Darby, reiterated his belief that CAF ought to continue to fight for African power within FIFA to gain "the place which is ours by right and which would allow us to play the role of a real respected partner and not that of a puppet."

Few have done more to propel Africa towards its proper place in world soccer than Tessema. **pi**

A BRAND HISTORY OF THE
EUROPEAN CHAMPIONSHIP

JL MURTAUGH

JANUARY 23RD 2010

Mountains. Flowers. Hearts. Stars. No, these are not elements of a new children's breakfast cereal – they are visual signifiers of the world's second-most prominent international football tournament. They also indicate the extent to which UEFA – and their local organizing committees – have commissioned ever-more elaborate and expensive brand identities to define the European Football Championship since 1996.

Graphic design has a captivating relationship to the game of football, particularly with regard to professional club identities developed or redefined in the modern era. The United States, in particular, had a great many adventurous insignias created in the late sixties and seventies for its brand-new soccer teams;

unshackled from the burden of history, tradition, and ethnic association.

Teams including the San Francisco Gales, New York Cosmos or Atlanta Apollos adopted minimal identities clearly inspired by the style of modernist graphic artist Paul Rand – largely regarded as the father of modern corporate design. The adoption of this aesthetic showed an ambitious vision to lay lasting and professional foundations in North America. A patently patriotic and singular visual manifesto, here the ideals of American corporate mobility were cunningly applied to sport.

Of course, these homegrown design methods were actually German, Swiss, and Dutch in origin; and Paul Rand was actually Peretz Rosenbaum, son of immigrant Jews in Brooklyn. Yet, such is design; so often maintaining an oxymoronic nature. Paradoxically, the most meticulous work is usually the simplest, and a successful solution can have almost any ideology grafted onto it after the fact.

THE 1960 LOGO
(AND 64, 72, 76, 80, 84, 88 AND 92)

From the same classic modernist era as Rand, the European Nations Cup was born in 1960. True to the time, a simple icon was created for the competition held in France, holding to the very definition of cool graphic minimalism. A rising wave of five lines in the national colors (two red, one white, two blue) over the confederation initials (a conjoined E/F following the same waveform) creates a fluttering flag symbolizing the international competition. And symbolize it, it did. This exact same icon was used for every tournament through 1992 in Sweden – with only the colors modified to reflect the changing host country, with two digits added to indicate the competition year.

An intriguing exception was the 1980 European Championship

in Italy, the second to be held in that country. While the officially recorded emblem was that same UEFA flag icon, the tournament organizers had developed a second: a flower with the familiar 32-panel "classic" football as its bloom, over the simple text EUROPA 80. While possibly looking like it belonged to a contemporary Atari video game, it did presage developments 12 years hence toward unique logos for each staging of the competition.

At this point, the tournament did not yet enjoy the high profile it now possesses, and fan interest/ financial support only hinted at the marketing behemoth the Euros have now become. Strangely, very little concrete information is actually available (publicly or otherwise) on the origins of European Championship identity prior to the 2004 tournament.

Consultation with reference material, design historians, and UEFA Media Services all led nowhere – in fact, correspondence with UEFA acknowledged their media archives do not even attempt to record and save such data. What follows, then, is an assessment of the tournament's recent brand development, with the benefit of the limited source materials available.

EURO96
ENGLAND

This was the tournament where I first became aware of the European Championships, thanks to coverage on ESPN and family interest in the exploits of the Spanish national team. The tournament was entertaining, Spain's shirts were "all-time" gorgeous, and inscribed on it all was the now famous Euro 96 logo.

Looking back, it was certainly an appropriate icon for the times, being an image that as easily could have served as cover art for a Blur single. Yet I recall having little idea what it was supposed to depict. It was clearly an abstract soccer ball, yes, but why was it drawn so strangely?

It was only well after the tournament that its representation became clear: an abstract football player, dribbling against a blue sky, under a yellow sun. Even now, it does seem a curious image given the extended period England went without hosting a major event, and all the possibilities for imagery therein.

Now, the typography beneath is far more successful, partly for existing before UEFA dropped its half-moon corporate wordmark into everything with which it was

associated. The lettering is tight, smart, and simple while maintaining a playfulness through a mixed but harmonious selection of typefaces.

All the necessary information is there in just 18 characters: who, what, where, and when. Notably, this was the first tournament officially referred to with the "Euro" abbreviation. Different naming directions might have been explored – but what prevailed, thankfully, showed a predilection to the succinct.

EURO2000
BELGIUM/NETHERLANDS

Where Euro96 was available on ESPN, I remember watching Euro2000 via pirated signals at restaurants. Characteristically, it featured prolonged Spanish disappointment, but also the best match I'd witnessed to that point in my life: Spain 4-3 Yugoslavia. I thought Gaizka Mendieta was beyond incredible, and Fernando Morientes claimed my most-favored-player status from Raul (for a time).

The logo barely registered. Maybe I didn't see it often enough, or perhaps this just wasn't an inclination I'd yet developed. Upon reflection, it is a very unsatisfactory emblem, doubly so as a representation for two paragons of creative design in Belgium and The Netherlands. The merging of the two countries' flags is a solid enough conceptual foundation from which to draw, but the execution lacks anything truly aesthetically unique to the region, one rich with inspirational creativity – ranging widely from Victor Horta's natural ornamentation to Theo van Doesburg's stark essentialism.

The typography used is even worse. The half-moon UEFA mark appropriately reflects the sphere above, but a bland serif titling adds nothing to the mark. The use of the same character for 0 and O further makes the lettering heavy to the right side. The presence of those four 0s normally might spark some creative handling of their juxtaposition, but in this instance it was a path un-pursued. All in all, a disappointing and ultimately forgettable image.

EURO2004
PORTUGAL

The competition was wonderful, the stadiums spectacular, the atmosphere magnificent, the logo atrocious. Lord knows how many tones, gradients, filters and blurs were employed to execute the 'official' version of the mark. It's interesting that now, most records have chosen to archive the "simplified" version produced for merchandise and printing purposes instead of using the Photoshop bonanza.

Reference materials from the logo unveiling claim "passion" as the unifying design principle (thus justifying the heart shape), as if passion was unique to Portugal. The base concept of a heart drawn around a ball is weak alone; but unneeded additions, complications and blends further obscures whatever rationale that wasn't actually there in the first place.

On the other hand, the typography is somewhat successful and productively keeps with the theme such as it is. The "PORTUGAL" tag does appear to be an afterthought, once they realized nothing about the image indicated where the tournament was actually taking place. There are certainly problems with character kerning and the fluidity between glyphs in the title (rendered as if it were a handwritten script) but these concerns largely pale against the atrocity residing above it.

EURO2008
AUSTRIA/SWITZERLAND

A tournament, once more, that was widely televised in the United States. My brief residency in Italy the year prior had permitted travel around the continent, and for the first time I'd actually been to nearly every city and stadium in the competition. I recall poking my head between the gates at Basel's St Jakob-Park, or sneaking into the unguarded upper tier of Vienna's Ernst-Happel-Stadion during an Austria Wien training session. Now, here they were hosting many of the biggest names in sport.

Of course, Spain's triumph will be my primary remembrance through future years, but the logo is much more along the lines of what one might expect visually from the two countries. A single line curving around a ball, rendered in red (their common national color) and green, with the line beveled and spiked to represent the primary topographical feature for which the nations are known – the Alps. While the use of shine and gradient is often overdone, it's subtle enough here to be effectual. The light reflection on the lower swoop even gives the feeling of a Alpine skier or bob-sledder racing to the finish.

The style and implementation of type below is exactly what you'd envision representing the Swiss. Simple, unadorned, sans-serif. A change in line weight to set off segments of information, compact leading, and precise attention to detail are its hallmarks. Even the location identifier is subtly aligned to the inner edges of the second-outermost characters. Overall, though it possesses a bit more shine and polish than necessary, it's still a winning result.

EURO2012
POLAND/UKRAINE

This brings us to the recently revealed Euro2012 logo, the first such competition to be held in Eastern Europe. Co-hosted by Poland and the Ukraine (two countries one might not otherwise think of together) it's sure to be the most publicized yet in the United States; while it's more likely than not I'll be watching from elsewhere, if not in person.

The European Championship is a genuine brand now, a mark of excellence and quality known around the world. The logo is more important than ever, but only as part of an overall brand identity carrying through every aspect of the tournament's presentation. Colors, graphics, and typeface – the Euro brand is now a complete experience. Everything from the press packets, to the façade of the Olimpiysky's VIP box (where the champion will receive the Delaunay Trophy) will have been designed along set identity guidelines.

Still, the logo is the most visible manifestation of the brand, and this one succeeds. Faced with the challenging task of creating an image common to countries not normally associated together, wildlife and the decorative arts served as fertile inspiration. While still possessing a "made-for-television" appearance via the use of delicate color blends not reproducible in other applications, it remains more restrained than most. Blooms in the nations' respective colors stem from a white and gold ball-plant, not wholly unlike the aforementioned unofficial Europa 80 mark. Figures illustrating celebrating players or cheering fans subtly jump from the petals of each.

The typography below might be its major triumph. The UEFA mark is set against the curve of the lower Ukrainian stem, and directly above the Euro "O". The lettering is built around this central axis, fluidly joining the R to the O, and using a lighter weight face for the year matching the curves around the UEFA mark. Much like the previous tournament, the location identifier is tight and balanced in the same style as the rest, feeling considered and part of the overall scheme.

For all its obtuse bureaucracy, UEFA has still shown attentiveness to branding and design appropriate to its European focus – a virtue that FIFA, on the other hand, has clearly been unable to adopt. Though often too complex, the newer Champions League branding alongside an annually renewed finals' identity are additional indicators of UEFA's keen visual awareness.

Unfortunately, recent World Cups, with the possible exception of the 2002 tournament in Korea/Japan, have had grossly deficient identities wholly unsuited to the most prominent sporting event on the planet. The South Africa 2010 logo is just the most recent atrocity. While on one hand FIFA have shown a predilection to contemporary arts, with initiatives to bring aboard global creatives for tournament poster designs, perhaps one day soon FIFA will give its crown jewel its deserved aesthetic attention. **pi**

CULTURE

GLORY, GLORY TOTTENHAM HOTSPUR

THE BATTLE HYMN OF THE REPUBLIC

JENNIFER DOYLE

FEBRUARY 3ʳᵈ 2008

THIS IS THAT unusual topic which allows me to indulge my passion for football, and, well, the passion that got me my day job teaching 19th century American literature.

If you are lucky enough to visit White Hart Lane on matchday, you might hear the Tottenham fans chant "Glory, Glory Tottenham Hotspur" to the tune of the song popularly known as "The Battle Hymn of the Republic." This is a typical patriotic American song – the sort of thing one hears sung over a loudspeaker at a fireworks display on July 4th, or belted out by a High School marching band around Thanksgiving. The Mormon Tabernacle Choir, for example, does a nice and sober version of this patriotic melody. It was weird to hear Spurs fans rooting on their team with the music from this popular but certainly staid American anthem. Almost as weird (and weirdly moving) as hearing Liverpool fans sing "You'll Never Walk Alone" – a song from the Rogers & Hammerstein musical Carousel – popularized by singers like Anita Bryant, Doris Day and Judy Garland. And let's not forget Jordan Sparks, who belted it out for American Idol.

MINE EYES HAVE SEEN THE GLORY

You have to understand: for those of us raised outside the UK, there's something fundamentally incongruous about the idea of Liverpool fans knowing the words to a song from Carousel. Inspired by a song she'd heard Union soldiers sing, Julia Ward Howe wrote the lyrics for "The Battle Hymn of the Republic" in 1861. Many of you will know at least the first two lines of the opening stanza:

Mine eyes have seen the glory
Of the coming of the Lord;
He is trampling out the vintage
Where the grapes of wrath are
stored;
He hath loosed the fateful lightning
Of His terrible swift sword;
His truth is marching on.

As loaded with images of God's wrath as it is, this is a neutral, 'cleaned' up version of the original song sung by Union soldiers marching into battle during the Civil War. Then it was known as "John Brown's Body" (also known as "John Brown's Song"). (PBS has a great web page with audio clips & text about its origin, and University of Virginia professor Franny Nudelman has written the book about this stuff.)

There are different versions of the song lyrics – but here's a simple one that gives you a sense of its peculiar, and peculiarly moving images:

John Brown's body lies a-mouldering
in the grave,
John Brown's body lies a-mouldering
in the grave,
But his soul goes marching on.
Chorus:
Glory, glory, hallelujah,

Glory, glory, hallelujah,
His soul goes marching on.
He's gone to be a soldier in the Army
of the Lord,
He's gone to be a soldier in the Army
of the Lord,
His soul goes marching on.
Chorus:
John Brown's knapsack is strapped
upon his back,
John Brown's knapsack is strapped
upon his back,
His soul goes marching on.
Chorus:
John Brown died that the slaves
might be free,
John Brown died that the slaves
might be free,
His soul goes marching on.
Chorus:
The stars above in Heaven now are
looking kindly down,
The stars above in Heaven now are
looking kindly down,
His soul goes marching on

Other versions have more complex lyrics – like:

He captured Harper's Ferry with his
nineteen men so true
He frightened old Virginia till she
trembled through and through
They hung him for a traitor, them-
selves the traitor crew
His soul is marching on.

Or,

Oh, soldiers of freedom, then strike
while strike you may

The deathblow of oppression in a bet-
ter time and way;
For the dawn of old John Brown was
brightened into day,
And his truth is marching on.

The song became, as evidenced by the above lyrics, a popular vehicle for celebrating the story of John Brown the abolitionist – a white man who was so opposed to slavery that he took up arms and led a raid on Harper's Ferry, a munitions facility – an arsenal, in fact. (No kidding!) His aim was to set an example with a successful raid that would lead to massive internal rebellion against the slave-holding governments of the southern states. The raid failed, and John Brown and his comrades were hanged by the US government.

MARCHING SONG

Amazing, then, that only a few years later soldiers fighting "to preserve the union" would honor a man executed by the government for trying to start a civil war. John Brown's story is one of the most fascinating in American history – it is, however, not often taught in schools. One can imagine why – because in telling that story, we find ourselves confronted by ugly truths about how violently the United States committed itself to slavery, and for how long.

From this point in history, John Brown's raid looks like the right thing to do: but it raises the question as to why more people didn't throw their lot in with those held in bondage.

Today, he is largely remembered as a religious fanatic.

Anyway, it is without a doubt one of the all time great political songs. Not in its melodic beauty – JBB is undoubtedly mind numbing, relentlessly repetitive. But it's thus a marching song well suited to Spurs fans who (and you know I love you) can't seem to do better than sing "Come On You Spurs" or "If You Hate Arsenal, Stand Up" – over and over again. "John Brown's Body" is up there with "Strange Fruit" as one of those songs that changed the world.

It is a song with a crazy history – and it is a song about crazy history. Once you know who John Brown was, why he fought and why he was hanged, when you hear that music you can't but feel a certain crazy determination in your bones to just get out there and make something happen. *Audere est Facere* indeed.

So, in the end, "John Brown's Body" has a meaning very similar to "You'll Never Walk Alone". It means something like: Everyone else in the living world might think you are crazy – but we'll follow you even if it means following you to our graves, knowing that we have righteousness on our side as we do so. Especially if you are taking on Arsenal. **pi**

SHALL WE SING A SONG FOR YOU

ITALIAN FOOTBALL SONGS

PART ONE

VANDA WILCOX

FEBRUARY 9ᵀᴴ 2008

Jennifer Doyle's interesting post on Tottenham Hotspur and the Battle Hymn of the Republic got me thinking about the kind of songs we sing here in Italy. Music is such a powerful force that the singing is often one of the most direct emotional aspects of going to football. When you go to any match in a country where you don't speak the language, it's very easy to feel excluded. After all, even if at home you wouldn't join in another team's chants, you would at least understand them. But of course each country has its own traditions when it comes to football songs, a mix of the familiar and the bizarre, and it can take time to learn your way around.

The first major difference from the English game is that nearly all clubs have their own official Hymn. This isn't a song which has been adopted, in the fashion of "You'll Never Walk Alone", but a specially written dedicated piece, usually by some prominent singer-songwriter who is a fan of the club in question. And they are almost without exception spectacularly cheesy, both musically and lyrically.

Though I am of course entirely biased, I think that Roma has one of the best, but Inter's is not too bad (and has the merit of acknowledging the team's inconsistency in its chorus "Crazy Inter" – a new celebratory version was recorded last year). The hymns of Lazio, Juve, Milan and Napoli are perhaps more representative of the typical awfulness of most such efforts. The lyrics are essentially banal sentimentalism of the laziest kind expressed with a sprinkling of local dialect, accompanied by cheesy europop beats and a climactic modulation to create a sense of emotional elevation. But if it's your team and your anthem, it is almost guaranteed to give you goose-bumps when belted out by 40,000 people.

There's no compunction about stealing other people's national anthems, either. The *Marseillaise*, curiously enough, gets used from time to time, and you'll also hear John Brown's body – the Battle Hymn of the Republic – usually known to Italians as "Glory Glory Hallelujah." It's sung at Lazio, as "Forza Forza Grande Lazio" and on the other side of the fence as, you'll be amazed to hear, "Forza Forza Grande Roma".

Some groups are also unable to resist the compelling tune of the Red Flag, even when they violently disagree with its political sentiments. British visitors will find plenty of other familiar tunes – rather bastardised versions of "Sailing", "Bread of Heaven", "Guantanamera" and so on. Meanwhile Roma sing anti-Lazio songs to the tune of Don't Cry for Me Argentina, the Popeye theme tune and best of all, Old Macdonald Had a Farm. Verdi is always a favourite, with both "La Donna è mobile" and the triumphal march from Aida cropping up across the country.

The international language of cheesy pop is of course a major source of musical inspiration. OMD's "Enola Gay", "That's the way I like it" by KC and the Sunshine band and of course "Go West" are universal favourites, while several clubs also use "Yellow Submarine". Plenty of classic Italian pop songs also get an airing. I often have the disconcerting experience of learning a song in the *curva* and only subsequently hearing the original version (which is usually a terrible disappointment). Juve sing a version of "Andavo a 100 al ora", a 1962 hit by Gianni Morandi which is great, while Marcella Bella's 1972 song from the San Remo festival of Italian song "Montagne Verde" is also used at Reggina and elsewhere. The shock of encountering Raffaella Carrà's 1978 masterpiece "Quanto è bello fare l'amore" in a tacky nightclub was considerable given that I had only ever heard a rather different version asserting that "there's no priest or woman for me, in my heart is only you: AS Roma".

New tunes are picked up from the charts or often from adverts on TV: the "kinder chocofresh music" (Inter), the "Grana Padano parmesan advert" (Roma). And of course fans borrow from one another. In February 2006 Roma played away at Bruges in the UEFA cup. The visiting fans were impressed by the Bruges' supporters use of the White Stripes' "Seven Nation Army" and the following week back home they adapted it to their own ends: PO-PO-PO-PO-PO-POOOO-POOO, making an anti-Lazio modification by adding "biancazzurro bastardo" [blue and white bastard] to the end. It became a Roma favourite in no time but quickly spread beyond to become the theme of Italy's 2006 World Cup campaign (without, obviously, the anti-Lazio addition). Roma, of course, abandoned it once it became associated with the Azzurri.

If the tunes are a combination of the familiar and the more obscure, the words cover more or less the same themes as football chants the world over. In two-club cities, songs tend to exult the status of one particular club in the city. Juve fans sing "Torino, what a beautiful city! Torino is our city! Torino is black and white, and black and white it will always be!" (This song is mendacious on at least two counts). Chievo sing "We are not Hellas!

We are Chievo!" which I suppose is at least straight to the point. Sampdoria sing "We are Genova" while Genoa retort "How the fuck can anyone support Samp?"

Another universal theme is the impossibility of staying away from your club. Torino fans sing "Torino... always at your side... I know why I won't be staying home." At Empoli, it's "I'll never grow tired of you, you're the most beautiful thing there is," a statement which stretches the boundaries of credibility if you take a look at their defenders Richard Vanigli and Vittorio Tosto. For Cagliari, simple geography makes loyalty a bit more demanding: they sing "We'll take the ship and follow you." Genoa (and others) sing a song as if by a resentful girlfriend: "Why do you leave me alone every Sunday to go to the stadium to watch the match? Because... because I support Genoa alé alé!" comes the answer.

Of course, a major part of any club's songbook consists of chants against other teams. This links into the regional prejudice I've mentioned before, and will be the subject of my next post. **pi**

SINGING AGAINST THE ENEMY

ITALIAN FOOTBALL SONGS

PART TWO

VANDA WILCOX

FEBRUARY 21ST 2008

L AST TIME OUT I looked at some of the songs which Italian fans sing in support of their own teams. But we all know that it's just as much fun, if not more so, to insult the opposition: what the Italians call *cori contro*, songs against, are one of the most enduring and often funniest parts of fan culture. It's also one of the most potentially problematic – encouraging prejudice and hostility, even racism, and frequently containing allusions to violence.

Among all the hysterical media discourse on Italy's hooligan problem over the last twelve months, I have read few more absurd assertions than that by a journalist in an Italian daily paper, who claimed that "Violence is directly related to the singing of *cori contro* – in England nobody sings songs against the opposition any more." The English tradition of *cori contro* is of course alive and well, and I don't imagine that efforts to eradicate them over here will have any success either.

Most numerous, and most vitriolic, is the category of songs against one's direct derby rivals, but many of these are rather uninteresting, revolving around the general theme of "you're shit and we hate you." There are occasional flashes of comic genius though: Roma fans, who like to stigmatise their Lazio rivals as ignorant country bumpkins, once threatened during the derby "We're going to steal your flock of sheep." Meanwhile Treviso threaten their rivals Venezia that "We'll burn *La Fenice* [the famous Venetian theatre] and chuck you in the canal."

Clubs' symbols are fair game for insult: the Roman wolf

is berated with various songs asserting "you're not wolves but just bastard dogs." And so are clubs' owners: an anti-Milan song attacks owner Silvio Berlusconi and Canale 5 (one of his Mediaset TV channels) along with a more familiar symbol of the *rossoneri*, Gianni Rivera. Meanwhile the classic anti-Juve chant insults both the fans and the club's owners, the FIAT-owning Agnellis: "On a Monday morning, what humiliation, going to the factory to serve your boss; Oh Juventino, you suck the dicks of the entire Agnelli family."

Juve are notorious for having fans from across Italy, especially in the South: Cagliari sing "Sardinian Juventino, you're even shittier than the ones from Torino."

Juve themselves sing what I am forced to admit is quite a funny ditty at the expense of Inter, who in 2001-02 thought they had won the Scudetto only to throw it away at the last minute in a hilarious fashion by losing at Lazio. The *bianconero* song, entitled "5 May 2002" runs as follows:

The fifth of May went rather badly
For Moratti and Internazionale
You were all in Rome, expecting
Celebrations, but forgetting
That the league is won in May

Not in July's dreamy days,
And while there were tears from
Ronie
Bianconeri began to party
And think of all you interisti
Down in Rome all sad and twisted
Oh interista, you know what we'll
do?
Put our hands in the air and sing for
you...
INTER MERDA, INTER MERDA
(OK, this is my first and last effort at retaining some kind of poetry in the translation).

Inter can retaliate very simply by taunting Juventus with "Serie B" – Inter are now the only club never to have played outside the top flight.

There are of course some deeply unpleasant chants around. Italy has its own equivalent of the Munich air disaster, and very similar opposition songs attached to it. The Superga tragedy of May 1949, in which 31 people including 18 players were killed returning from a European game against Benfica, devastated Torino in a way which Munich could not destroy Manchester United. Sadly this is today acknowledged by rival chants about "that magical aeroplane".

Incidentally, for Toro's 50th anniversary in 1999 they held a friendly against an all-star Italian

League XI. I wouldn't like to gamble on the likely consequences had the Turin derby fallen that week, but I'm not sure Juve would have behaved as well as Man City fans did, since they sing that "you only made history at Superga."

A large proportion of *cori contro* are aimed less at a specific club, than at a city or a region. Some chants are generic and multipurpose, like the old favourite "Roman/Milanese/Torinese/Catanese mothers are whores" or simply "Odio Bergamo" (I hate Bergamo) or Napoli or Genoa or any other three-syllable placed name which can be made to scan (Manchester, for instance). Insults can apply to whole regions. Tuscany has the most clubs of any region in Serie A, so a one-size fits all approach is useful: "Tuscan women are whores, whores, whores, and their sons are rabbits, rabbits, rabbits." The rabbit is a traditional emblem of cowardice.

Sampdoria fans get told "Genova stinks of fish and its sea is polluted" (part of the Italian ultras' well-known campaign for cleaner beaches, perhaps.) Meanwhile fans of the Milan and Turin clubs are taunted over their bad weather: to the tune of Guantanamera, "Solo la nebbia! Avete solo la nebbia!" – only fog,

you only have fog. Not something for which any part of the British Isles could safely mock any other area.

Violence is frequently present in these songs – not that many people are likely to actually have the hand-grenade suggested in the short rhythmic chant "Bomba a mano su Milano!" Roma fans suggest that Milan should be torched – "Milano in fiamme" – while Juve fans sing exactly the same song but substituting Florence in flames.

But it's Napoli, and Naples as a city, which really bears the brunt of regional prejudice. "Come on Vesuvius, clean them with fire" is a typical sentiment, while local rivals Cavese update things slightly by urging Osama Bin Laden to direct his plane towards Napoli Central Station. Meanwhile the classic chant runs:

Smell what a stench, even dogs flee
The Neapolitans are arriving
O cholera and earthquake-afflicted
You've never seen soap in your lives
Napoli are shit, Napoli [have]
cholera
you're the shame of all Italy,
Neapolitan, dirty African
Sooner or later we'll stab you.

This delightful ditty combines all the worst stereotypes about Naples – poverty, dirt, disease

– with a garnishing of racism
and violence to boot. Though it's
not only northerners who look
on those south of them with
contempt. Bari fans, safe in the
knowledge that they are all of
150km north of their hated rivals,
call Lecce fans "Africans."

If this is indeed irony, I struggle to appreciate it myself. Given
that both Bari and Lecce are part
of the same region, this shows
how closely integrated racist and
localist discourse are. But by and
large, though, most *cori contro* stay
within the bounds of acceptability
and humour. **pi**

THE OLD, WEIRD EVERYWHERE

BRISTOL ROVERS AND "GOODNIGHT, IRENE"

BRIAN PHILLIPS

FEBRUARY 16TH 2008

LIKE MANY OF you, I've really enjoyed Jennifer's and Vanda's posts about football songs over the past couple of weeks, and I thought I'd add my own contribution with a look at the history of one of the strangest supporter songs in football – "Goodnight, Irene," an American folk song about love and suicide that's been the anthem of Bristol Rovers for almost 60 years.

Bristol Rovers Football Club and the musician known as Leadbelly were both born in the 1880s, but – for a while, at least – they both had different names. The football club was founded by a 19-year-old schoolteacher in 1883 in a restaurant in one of England's major seaports; they happened to wear black kits, and to play on a pitch next to a rugby team called the Arabs, and to mark

both facts, they called themselves Black Arabs F.C. The musician was born, sometime around 1888, on a plantation near Mooringsport, Louisiana; he was named Huddie William Ledbetter – presumably to mark nothing at all.

Today, of course, Bristol Rovers are as associated with "Goodnight, Irene," Leadbelly's most famous recording, as any English club with any song. They've been singing it since the 1950s, a full decade before "You'll Never Walk Alone" was heard at Anfield, 30 years before Manchester City fans began to chant "Blue Moon."

But the path that led to the association was chancy and circuitous, and in many ways, both Rovers and Leadbelly are lucky that they survived long enough for the song and the club's fans to find each other.

Leadbelly lived through the old, weird America, as Greil Marcus would call it: deep swamp dance hall nights, brothels at St. Paul's Bottoms, hobos on freight trains, chain gangs, Satan at the cross-roads, impossible stars overhead. He was a "musicianer" as early as 1903, and learned in the red-light districts of riverboat towns to channel the mournful twang of American folk music into some-thing distinctive and personal, made from his clear voice and his oversized 12-string guitar. He drank rotgut and fought anyone, and his prowess at one or the other resulted in the nickname he would later take on stage.

He went to prison, not for the first time, in 1918 – for murder, after killing a man in a fight. He had a 35-year sentence, but was released just two years later after he wrote a song appealing to the governor for clemency. In 1930 he was in jail again, this time for attempted homicide; and it was here that he was discovered by John Lomax, the legendary musicologist, who traveled the country making recordings for the Archive of American Folk Song at the Library of Congress. With the help of another susceptible gover-nor, Lomax arranged Leadbelly's release, and recorded his versions

of hundreds of songs – including "Goodnight, Irene," an obscure number from the late nineteenth century that Leadbelly claimed to have learned from an uncle.

Black Arabs F.C. became Eastville Rovers in 1884, then Eastville Bristol Rovers in the late 1890s. In 1899, under their current name, they joined the Southern League, just in time for the great era of regional league play before the formation of the national Third Division. They were champions in 1905. During Leadbelly's first serious prison stint, they were suspended for the First World War; they reformed, and joined the Football League as members of the new Third Division, around the time he was released. They stayed afloat during the '30s, but signed a bad lease on their ground that would cause them trouble for decades, and finished last in the division in 1938-39.

The same year, Leadbelly was back in jail for assault. He'd struggled throughout the '30s to make a living, despite the expo-sure he won as a protégée of John Lomax; record companies tried to turn him into a blues singer, which never really suited his style. But he was out of jail in 1940, and found himself in Greenwich

Village just at the moment when the folk scene was forming: he befriended and influenced Woodie Guthrie and Pete Seeger, and experienced greater success in the 1940s than in any other decade of his life. He died in 1949, after falling ill during his first tour of Europe.

That same year, Pete Seeger's group, the Weavers, released a cover of "Goodnight, Irene" that spent 25 weeks on the Billboard charts, peaking at #1.

It was the Billboard Single of the Year, and was quickly covered by any number of other musicians, including Frank Sinatra.

It worked its way to England, where it reached Bristol and became, by the end of the 1950-51 season, one of the Rovers fans' favorite songs. There are any number of legends to explain the supporters' adoption of a plaintive and slightly mystical American folk melody as their anthem, a song whose lyrics don't exactly advertise their suitability for the purpose:

Sometimes I live in the country,
Sometimes I live in town,
Sometimes I take a great notion,
Jumpin' into the river and drown.

...

I love Irene, God knows I do,
Love her until the sea run dry,

And if Irene turns her back on me,
Gonna take morphine and die.

Possibly the most persuasive story is that Plymouth Argyle fans sang the song to taunt Rovers supporters after Argyle took the lead in a match. When Rovers went on to win 3-1, their fans turned the taunt around and began to sing "Goodnight, Argyle." And the song stuck. Something about it just fit.

I love thinking about the loose threads of beauty and meaning in this world and the way they sometimes come together in football. I love imagining Leadbelly playing in a smoky shack to an audience of hellhounds and moonshine runners while five thousand miles away a group of men with kestrel stares and pushbroom mustaches took the pitch in their high-waisted professional short pants. I love the way a game played by the children of lords and a suicide moan from the American folk tradition can make something bizarre and powerful today, something unifying, in a context that makes perfect sense to us, though it would baffle the people who invented them. **pi**

THE BEST?

FOOTBALL AS NEVER BEFORE

MARC BAHNSEN

MARCH 26TH 2010

IN LOOKING AT George Best *Fußball wie noch nie* ("Football as Never Before") it would be logical to set the work next to the more widely viewed 2006 film, *Zidane: A 21st Century Portrait* and analyze the similarities and differences. But, in my eyes, I don't think it would be fair to either film. There's no doubt the Zidane edition is a direct descendant of the 1971 work by German filmmaker Hellmuth Costard, with the exact same premise driving both the storyline and singular character focus. But where the two differ is outside the film itself – particularly, in the eyes of this viewer.

Anyone who has followed the game during the past decade and a half would need no introduction to Zidane. The player crowned as Best in the World (three or four iterations ago, depending on whom you ask) performed in the hyper-individualistic environment of the modern game, with super stardom fueling jersey sales and advertisements. Growing up in middle America long after Best had hung up his boots, and not a particular fan of Manchester United, my exposure to Best as the player was next to nil.

Contrarily, my perception of the Zidane film was already influenced by knowledge of his entire career, from the time I was first introduced to him in the '96-'97 Champions League final via a borrowed VHS tape from a middle school teammate, all the way through to the infamous incident in which he decided to mark the end of his career. I have to only assume that the era and football world Best played in was far different from that of Zidane, but that Best played a major part in the existence of the modern football superstar. So what follows is a raw attempt to interpret Best as the player and what he brought to the game, technically, through the limited focus of the six camera lenses. (The film is rarely screened in the United States, but I was lucky enough to catch it recently at an indie filmhouse in Chicago.)

The film flyer set the tone, Football as Never Before was a work that followed "the mercurial George Best" for an entire 90 minutes of a 1970 match between Manchester United and Coventry City. In absolute terms, a camera following George Best for 90 minutes is exactly what we were treated to. But it is the "mercurial" nature of George Best that allowed a football aficionado to derive more of his footballing lore from only the limited view of what met the eye. Whether he was out wide on the left letting loose raking balls towards the final third, or at the corner of his own 18 beginning a counter-attack, there was an immediately apparent higher quality to everything surrounding Best. This quality is somehow different than the word "quality" we loosely throw around describing players or the game today. This sort of quality, in the most literal sense, is the type that words do no justice to, the one that sets players possessing a rarefied singular talent apart from the rest of the pack. The once-in-a-generation quality, if you will.

This being my first exposure to any sort of extended footage of Best in action, his talent was instantly recognizable and the impression left on my mind was a lasting one. Such was his life that, as a twenty-something football junkie, I knew far more about his off-the-field exploits than the specific skills he possessed while on it. And those skills were nothing short of brilliant. Once again, a word that is thrown around so much these days to the point where it's nearly devoid of its meaning, but brilliance seems well suited to sum up the play of Best. Watching the film I had to think back to the Northern Irish phrase "Maradona good, Pelé better, George Best" and wonder if it wasn't something more than just an exaggerated witty colloquialism.

Languid, yet not lazy – extremely quick, but still efficient with his runs – he held the ball well under pressure, while not afraid to get stuck in himself – and had that shared quality that all the Greats possess, a true vision of the game which allowed him to stay one step ahead of the pace. Yes, perhaps it is a stretch to ascertain so much of the player and his importance to the team while watching with such a limited viewpoint, but I think in a way this restricted profile only magnified his incredible talents.

By my count, there were only two or three legitimate tackles where Best lost the ball, and to the credit of Coventry City players in this match, they were well-timed and well-executed tackles. It seemed that only such would do to dispossess the ball from the feet of Best. Weaker challenges were shrugged aside, and even if they were momentarily successful, Best was quick to regain possession of the ball and continue the play forward. His sublime approach looked cool under pressure, as Best was never hurried and decisive with his actions.

If we only relied on the limited frame of the picture, it would indeed make it hard to say he was certainly playing the right ball... but this conclusion we owe to the Old Trafford faithful. Often times in the middle/attacking third the ball Best played forward would eventually be met with a collective sigh from the crowd, followed by applause – which leads us to

assume that the ball went on to be part of a chance (or near-chance) on goal. An interesting way of deducing the end product, but at the same time it was a pleasure to see Best observe the play he orchestrated.

His pace was blistering, but what impressed the most was how quickly he reached that top gear. At the drop of a coin, Best was off and flying down the flank in support of an attack, or starting the attack itself. Numerous times Best dropped into the middle of the pitch to receive the ball around the center circle, turned and off he went. The turn, in many instances, was where the beauty of his play truly shone through. Almost as an afterthought, he changed the direction of the ball with his thigh or outside of the boot and was off and running. He had the mind to look for what was next, while making the turn with an effortlessly second nature-like approach, while a lesser being may have been caught up in the turn itself and fault all that followed. After the turn, how the ball stayed glued to his foot as he slalomed past defenders was another element of wonder.

Best had obviously mastered the simple drop of his shoulder to leave challengers yards behind scrambling in a futile attempt to catch him. We were lucky enough to see this move executed to ultimate perfection, as 10 minutes into the second half Best dribbled a few defenders to leave him one-on-one with the Coventry keeper. The ball ever-attached to his boots, the keeper came to meet Best at the top of the box. At full speed, Best merely suggested of a dipping shoulder feint to the right, and the goalie went to ground with the intention of getting the ball, Best, or both. None troubled by this mortal creature in his path, as the prey bit hard on the feint to the right Best simply cut the ball across to his left and he was left well alone for a tap-in. All the while so eloquently executed.

The workrate George Best displayed was perhaps the most surprising thing to me about the film. The idea of him as a glamorous footballer, even the first glamour footballer, led me to believe I would be watching a somewhat relaxed player spraying passes around the pitch as he pleased. Much to discredit my thoughts, Best worked tirelessly to receive the ball, in the build-up and during the attack, as well as the occasional tracking run on defense. One sequence showed Best dispossess the opposition near his own 18, and go on a rampaging run for a good 40-50 yards as the people in the front rows of the terrace blurred in the background, releasing an unseen player, followed by an assumed near-missed opportunity and a round of applause a few seconds later. The second goal of the match was scored in a similar fashion, where Best beat a few defenders, unleashed a shot towards goal…and after a presumed botched effort by the goalkeeper or a Coventry defender, Best is running towards his teammates in celebration. And 2-0 is the way it ended.

There are some points during the match that he appears to be standing around, but never is it in a disinterested fashion. To the unaware eye this may be interpreted as laziness, but it would be foolish for any player to be running for the full 90 minutes. Even in his idle moments, Best was keenly aware of the right moment to unleash a flying run on the side, or when to come to and receive the ball. He even cracks a smile here and there, leaving us only wondering what could be playing out on the rest of the pitch.

Later on this workrate and pace must have dwindled, accelerated no doubt by his social excesses off the pitch, so it was a blessing that we have this game preserved while he was still fully fit. It's not hard to imagine Best still dominating without the pace, though, as this was clearly not the only aspect of his game. One of the first clips I can recall of Best in his later years showed he had kept that mastery of the dribble after his physical prowess was on the decline.

Judging from where Best was filmed most often, United were the better side and Coventry appeared to rarely threaten the opposing goal. This experience was not really one of watching the game itself, but it was the act of seeing the game through the eyes of a genius that gave us an understanding of what was happening on the pitch. To be so focused on a single player for the entire game carries the inherent risk of monotony, but with Best the dull points are carried as an exercise of watching a man operate in his natural surroundings. The focused cameras give us an opportunity to get an almost primordial feel of what is like to see the game as a top class footballer...and a legend who shaped the groundwork for the lifestyle and scrutiny afforded to those superstars that followed after his playing days were long gone. **pi**

THE ROUGH GUIDE TO
FOOTBALL IN PRINT

ALEX USHER

AUGUST 27TH 2010

A FEW WEEKS ago, Tom Dunmore asked me to be Pitch Invasion's regular book reviewer even though he knew full well my blogging track record is just this side of abysmal (I am, to the half-dozen of you who read my work, the blogger known as Antonio Gramsci). I was so flattered I actually accepted but ever since, I've been fretting over what to write my first column about, not least because I haven't actually read a football book other than the amply-reviewed *Beckham Experiment* in several months and my next fix from Amazon. co.uk probably won't show up for another couple of weeks. So, what to write about? How can I introduce myself to the Pitch Invasion faithful?

In the end I decided that if I'm going to be regaling you all with my take on football books on a regular basis, I should probably start with an overview of the state of football literature in general. After all, it's back-to-school time, and I'm sure you're eager to do the background reading before we begin our journey together through the coming year's football books.

THE BASICS

Lets start with the basics: as in every genre of sports writing, the mainstay is the biography or auto-biography of the superstar player. These are normally tedious; the only ones which are vaguely of interest are the ones where the player himself is or was horribly messed-up in some way – Tony Adams'*Addicted*, for instance, or Jimmy Burns' biography of

Maradona, *The Hand of God: The Life of Diego Maradona*. If anything, football lags behind other sports in this area: there has yet to be a player autobiography of the standard of Ken Dryden's *The Game*, or that has the humour of Bill Lee's *The Wrong Stuff*. This is not, in truth, entirely the fault of the publishing industry. Football doesn't really produce many intellectuals on Dryden's level (the only one I can think of off the top of my head would be Jorge Valdano, who does in fact write books on football, but none of them have been translated into English), and while it does have its share of "characters", it's hard to think of any quite as colourfully anarchic as Lee, either. Chalk it up, perhaps, to the limitations of the sporting culture rather than of the publication culture.

Biographies aren't limited to players: managers and occasionally referees get a look-in, too. Again, there's nothing here to look at, really.

After player biographies come club biographies – these, too are usually dreck. Read one on your own team, by all means. If you want more, read Phil Ball's *White Storm: The Story of Real Madrid* about Real Madrid, which is probably the best of this genre and maybe Jimmy Burns' *Barca: A*

People's Passion (although the latter needs to be taken with a serious dose of salt). Do yourself a favour and give the rest a miss. There simply aren't enough teams with world-historical importance even within the limited terms of the football world. Books which look at "big derbies" aren't much better, often reducing major clubs to outdated stereotypes (e.g. bourgeois River Plate vs. proletarian Boca Juniors) in order to build up the story.

THE FOOTBALL BUSINESS

Football is, increasingly, a business – and there's any number of books about how money (usually personified in the form of Sky's owner Rupert Murdoch) is ruining football. Most are pretty uninteresting, but David Conn's books *The Football Business: Fair Game in the '90s?* and *The Beautiful Game?: Searching the Soul of Football* both mix excellent financial reporting with a fierce and passionate devotion to the welfare of the fans who support the game. They're well worth a read.

Of course, corruption isn't just about business – it's in the buying and selling of matches, a subject examined in Declan Hill's recent book *The Fix: Soccer and*

Organized Crime. And there's also a long history of serious corruption allegations at FIFA headquarters itself in Lausanne, Switzerland. A quick read of journalist Andrew Jennings' *Foul!: The Secret World of FIFA: Bribes, Vote Rigging and Ticket Scandals* is the best way to get a handle on this, though more academically-minded readers may prefer John Sugden and Alan Tomlinson's books *FIFA and the Contest for World Football: Who Rules the Peoples' Game* and *Badfellas: FIFA Family at War*, or Paul Darby's *Africa, Football and FIFA: Politics, Colonialism and Resistance.*

Academically minded, you say? Is there really an academic literature on football? You bet. Some of it is quite good (though since it's priced at academic rates, it's not the most accessible literature in the world). Most of the really good stuff is either written or edited by the University of Aberdeen's Richard Giulianotti, and his *Football: A Sociology of the Global Game* is well worth the investment for the serious-minded. Also worth a look is *Football and Fascism: The National Game under Mussolini*, a book adapted from author Simon Martin's University College London PhD thesis.

FEVER PITCH AND BEYOND

One of the problems with football literature, you'll realize quickly, is that there is far, far too much of it about. Often, sub-genres start promisingly but then die a horrible death as someone tries to replicate the same theme for every single team in the Premiership and Football League. Nick Hornby's *Fever Pitch*, for instance, which was a well-written meditation on the relationship between sport, narrative and masculinity with Arsenal at its centre, was followed by at least thirty-odd volumes by fans writing books about their lives and how their fanatical support for (insert team here) is a metaphor for their overall condition in life. Dreck.

Another sub-genre is the "seasonal" genre. Some journalist comes up with an idea to spend a year following a particular team. Hunter Davies originally did it with Tottenham in the 1970s in his book *The Glory Game*; the concept was updated and given a bit of a twist in the 1990s when American author Joe McGuiness spent a season at a tiny Italian club in *The Miracle of Castel di Sangro: A Tale of Passion and Folly in the Heart of Italy*. These two books are classics and belong in everyone's library. Tim Parks' *A Season with Verona: Travels Around Italy in Search of Illusion, National Character, and...Goals!* had the literary style one would expect from a novelist and is an interesting look at the culture of Italian *tifosi* but ultimately kind of craps out because Parks' knowledge of football isn't brilliant. The couple of dozen other attempts at this genre, sometimes by journalists (like Guillem Balague's *A Season on the Brink: A Portrait of RAFA Benitez's Liverpool*), but more often usually by fans trying to find a way to write off the cost of their season ticket as a business expense (e.g. *The Great Divide: The Inside Story of the 1999-2000 Season at Arsenal and Tottenham Hotspur* by Alex Fynn and Olivia Blair). Unless you have an obsessive-bordering-on-compulsive interest in that particular club, they are not worth the paper they are printed on. And even then...

Then there's hoolie porn: endless reams of books, usually by ex-hooligans, talking about the fights they had, how hard such-and-such a firm is, etc. Or the related genre of books about the sordid world that revolves around footballers, such as Mirror journalist Graham Johnson's *Football and Gangsters:*

How Organised Crime Controls the Beautiful Game. These can almost all be filed under "books that make you feel dirty when you read them". Read Bill Buford's *Among the Thugs*, by all means, or John Sugden's *Scum Airways: Inside Football's Underground Economy* (which recounts how the hooligan element came to dominate the football tourism trade and the fake replica shirt market). Other than that, steer clear.

Books about specific historical incidents are occasionally worthwhile, and there are a lot of good books about the period around World War Two, including David Downing's *Passovotchka: Moscow Dynamo in Britain, 1945* (the Red Army team's 1945 tour of the UK), Andy Dougan's *Dynamo: Triumph and Tragedy in Nazi-Occupied Kiev* (about a semi-mythical game in occupied Ukraine where a team from Kiev beat a German Air Force team despite severe intimidation, after which several players were executed), and of course Simon Kuper's *Ajax, the Dutch, the War: Football in Europe During the Second World War* (which is about football during World War One in general, but more specifically about the fate of Jewish club members once German *judenrein* policies came into effect in the Netherlands in 1940).

THE GLOBAL GAME

Arguably, it was this same Kuper who inaugurated the modern age of football writing that started in the mid-1990s with the publication of *Soccer Against the Enemy: How the World's Most Popular Sport Starts and Fuels Revolutions and Keeps Dictators in Power*. Bits of it are now dated, and some of the stuff on South America and the Ukraine are a bit dubious (the part suggesting that Dynamo Kiev was exporting fissile material in the mid-90s strains credulity), but overall it's a fantastic read. Few have come close to equaling it – Franklin Foer's attempt at doing so in *How Soccer Explains the World: An Unlikely Theory of Globalization* was mostly pathetic apart from a decent essay on Serbian football. But it's nevertheless a historiographically important book because it opened up the eyes of the English reading public to the fact that football is a sociological window into the soul of other cultures.

This line of inquiry has led to a series of national histories of the game, and through it some of the best football writing around. David Winner's *Brilliant Orange: The Neurotic Genius of Dutch Football*, John Foot's *Calcio: A History of Italian Football*, Ulrich-Hesse Lichtenberger's *Tor!: The Story of German Football*, Alex Bellos' *Futebol: Soccer: The Brazilian Way*, Phil Ball's *Morbo: The Story of Spanish Football*, David Wangerin's *Soccer in a Football World: The Story of America's Forgotten Game* and Jonathan Wilson's *Behind the Curtain: Travels in Eastern European Football* are all excellent national/regional histories of football of Holland, Italy, Germany, Brazil, Spain, the United States and Eastern Europe, respectively.

The problem with this genre is that once someone has written about a country or an area, then it is "done" and that territory taken. And, to be blunt, we're running out of territory. James Montague took out most of the Arab world last year in a good-in-patches-but-disappointing-overall book *When Friday Comes: Football in the War Zone*. Ditto Russia, with Marc Bennett's *Football Dynamo: Modern Russia and the People's Game*. Steve Menary tried to outflank everyone by writing about football in non-nations – those islets and stateless ethnic groups that make up the non-FIFA world, such as Greenland, Tibet and Gibraltar

– in an engaging way in his book *Outcasts!: The Lands That FIFA Forgot,* even if his central premise that FIFA should chuck out any considerations about national sovereignty every time some groupuscule says it wants to field a football team is only barely this side of being totally batshit.

But the real problem with these geographically-centred histories of the game is that in many ways they were completely blown out of the water by the monumental and magisterial *The Ball is Round: A Global History of Soccer* by David Goldblatt. This frankly brilliant 915-page global history of football everywhere around the world has set the bar for football history so high that it's possible no one has anything left to say.

There's a similar problem with respect to tactics. Though historically a fringe area of football publication, you could occasionally find a half-decent book on the subject – Sky's Andy Gray published a surprisingly good book on tactics called *Flat Back Four* about a decade ago. But last fall, Jonathan Wilson published *Inverting the Pyramid: The History of Football Tactics,* and it's hard to imagine anyone ever bettering it as a description of the development of football formations. There

is probably still some room for a specialist tome on the evolution of defensive tactics, but other than that Wilson's book is it.

Rounding out the literature, of course, are the quirky books. Charlie Connelly following the Lichtenstein national team for two years of World Cup Qualification in *Stamping Grounds: Exploring Liechtenstein and Its World Cup Dream*; Andrew Anthony's history of spot-kicks in *On Penalties,* Musa Okwonga's take on the eleven elements of a successful footballer in *A Cultured Left Foot: The Eleven Elements of Footballing Greatness.* There's a few of these gems around, but if the title is going out of its way to scream quirky, it's usually not worth the hassle. Paul Brown's medley of anecdotes, published under the title *Balls: Tales from Football's Nether Regions,* is one of those examples of a book that had a title long before any text was actually written.

So where next for football literature? Is there anything useful left to write in the post-Goldblatt era? Well, there's a good deal more to be written about the economics of football. This has received some academic treatment and was touched on to a certain extent by Andrew Zimbalist and Stefan Szymanski in their comparative history of football and baseball *National Pastime.* Expect Szymanski to touch on this theme a bit more in his forthcoming book (already released in the UK) with Simon Kuper entitled *Why England Lose: and Other Curious Phenomena Explained,* which I'll be reviewing in the next couple of months.

Geographically speaking, a good treatment of African football is desperately needed – it's been done a couple of times by Peter auf der Heyde and Filippo Maria Ricci, but neither really gets to grips with the subject in a substantive way. Mexico and Argentina could both do with something solid on their domestic games and though a couple of authors have had a run at French football, it's still in need of a good popular treatment.

There's definitely room for a book on how people consume football, both historically and in the electronic age – the different varieties of fandom and spectatorship. I nominate Tom for this one. But most of all what football literature needs is some decent fiction. Apart from David Peace's *The Damned Utd,* a fictionalized account of Brian Clough's career and in particular his 44 days at the helm of Leeds United, there is remarkably little fiction of any quality at all dealing with our favourite sport. Certainly, football has yet to produce anything like the genius of W.P. Kinsella. With so much drama embedded in the game and the generally soap operatic nature of events off the pitch, it's hard to believe that the sport still trails baseball in this respect. But it seems there's no one on the horizon seeking to end this literary drought. **pi**

SOCCER EMPIRE

THE WORLD CUP AND THE FUTURE OF FRANCE

ALEX USHER

JULY 21ˢᵀ 2010

IT'S EASY TO be cynical about a book written by an American history professor which starts out describing the events of July 9ᵗʰ 2006. Oh shit, you think to yourself, it's John Doyle with a doctorate; another football outsider thinking his fresh set of eyes can derive some deeper social meaning from "The Beautiful Game" which the rest of us have somehow missed all these years. And there's going to be more drivel about the head-butt. I mean, please. Spare us.

Easy to be cynical, certainly, but in this case you'd be largely wrong. While Laurent Dubois' *Soccer Empire: The World Cup and the Future of France* as a whole can't be considered a great book – for reasons I'll delve into momentarily – it nevertheless contains passages of surpassing

excellence which makes it well worth delving into.

The book is a bit of a mishmash in that it is essentially three books in one. The first of these is an exploration of France's colonial history through sport and in particular football. Since Dubois is an historian, it's not surprising that this is by some distance the best of the three. In the space of about eighty pages, he manages to illuminate the long and tangled history of France's long relationship with its colonies in Algeria, West Africa and the Caribbean. In doing so, he illuminates the role of sport in the evolution of anti-colonial and anti-racism movements in ways that few have ever rivaled.

Basically, sports – and especially team sports – have always had a strong egalitarian streak because within the timeframe and rules of a given sport or event, any larger oppression or social influence disappears. When a team of black players plays a team of white players at any sport, regardless of what other power relationships might exist off the pitch, "superiority" between the two is determined by sheer individual or team ability (which is precisely why Hitler tried to stop Jesse Owens competing and why the colour barrier in baseball took so long to fall). It's partly for this reason that the agitation for racial equality has often had a sporting dimension; but it's partly also because football clubs share with political parties the ability to act as both a focus and a channel for collective emotions and desires. Dubois' exploration of this theme is nothing short of excellent.

Having made the general point about sport, equality and politics, he then goes on to describe the interplay between them in the course of the de-colonization of the French Empire. Especially poignant here is the biography of Félix Éboué, the black Guianan civil servant, who by one of those quirks of French history and politics rose so high in the colonial civil service that he became Governor of Martinique and then of Chad (though colonialism made a mockery of the words, *Liberté, Egalité, Fraternité,* they occasionally retained their meaning in some surprising ways, you see). History remembers him primarily as the man who rallied the French African colonies to the side of De Gaulle's Free French in 1940 (for which he was rewarded with burial in the Pantheon), but he also spent much of his career organizing greater sporting opportunities for his subjects in the Caribbean and as a result left a sporting infrastructure which would nourish many athletes who would eventually come to be the heart of French sport.

The second book lurking within the covers of *Soccer Empire* is really the weakest, and that is the history of French football, with a major emphasis on the period between 1998 and 2006. This part of the book starts off well, performing a particularly valuable service in dispelling the idea that the 1998 Black, *blanc, beur* team was an unprecedented breakthrough in multiculturalism. Dubois shows adroitly that in fact *Les Bleus* have been accommodating players from outside metropolitan France for over seventy years. North Africans (or their children) have been a mainstay of the

French national team since before World War Two and the first black was capped for *Les Bleus*, Raoul Diagne (whose father Blaise was the National Assembly member from Senegal), got his call up in 1931. Indeed, the first genuinely multi-cultural French team was not the one that won in Paris in 1998 but the one that was so cruelly defeated in Sevilla in 1982.

However, the closer the book comes to the present day, the less interesting it becomes. The descriptions of public reactions to both the joyous World Cup victory of 1998 and the bemusing loss of 2006 (capped as it was by Zinedine Zidane's iconic *coup de boulle*) are essentially collections of press clippings. The final chapter, an extended meditation of the possible meanings of Zidane's head-butt, is a particularly tedious summation of much of the pseudo-intellectual masturbation that followed France's defeat (for those genuinely interested in this subject, Ed Smith's *What Sports Tells Us About Life* offers a more succinct and believable explanation about what happened on 9 July 2006).

Less forgivably, the book contains enough niggling factual errors about the sport of football itself that it puts Dubois'

credentials as an actual football fan in some question. The Heysel stadium disaster, for instance, occurred in 1985, not 1983; the famous France-Brazil match of 1986 was a quarter-final, not a semi-final, and so on and so forth. Though it's not a hanging sin, the author is noticeably less comfortable with the actual sporting facts on the ground than he is with the nuances of colonial history.

Tying these two books together is a third book, which follows Zidane and Lilian Thuram in their life journey from the cities to the historic French teams of 1996-2006. From a narrative point of view, this makes a certain amount of sense: in the Black, *blanc, beur* squad, Zidane was the only *beur* and Thuram was arguably the most talented and certainly the most outspoken of the black players. Both scored two crucial goals on the road to the 1998 triumph (Thuram in the semi-final and Zidane in the final), and both retired briefly before being coaxed back into the fold for the 2006 World Cup. And both spent at least part of their childhood in the cites, Thuram in Paris and Zidane in Marseilles. Dubois can therefore use their childhoods to look at the condition of blacks and Arabs in modern France, while at the same time looking at how their sporting careers have helped to change perceptions about what constitutes Frenchness.

The problem with this last book is that it is uneven. While Thuram has gradually transcended his role as a footballer to take on the mantle of a political figure, Zidane's greater status as a footballing icon has never translated into a social role because he has never shown much interest in being political. Due to Zidane's silence, this third book is really just a long love letter to Thuram. In itself, that's not a bad thing: Thuram is genuinely one of the most intelligent and eloquent men alive on the subject of race and tolerance, and his repeated showdowns with Jean-Marie LePen, Nicolas Sarkozy and other law-and-order politicians in France are a joy to read.

But the imbalance within the third book unbalances the book as a whole. Having set up Thuram and Zidane as the twin ethnic pillars on which to make a narrative bridge between France's colonial history and the remarkable story of the French national team between 1998 and 2006, he has to give them equal time. When it comes to Thuram, it works well because he personally contributed not only to *Les Bleus* success but was also a major actor in the country's political evolution as well. But when it comes to Zidane…well, there was that headbutt, wasn't there? And right there, the narrative comes crashing down as Dubois gets pushed on to, as it were, his weaker foot and has to talk about the football rather than the politics.

This book is worth reading for its first couple of chapters on sport and politics and on France's complicated colonial history and its present-day reverberations, which are undoubtedly superb. And it's worth reading for a greater understanding of the brilliance and eloquence of Lilian Thuram (and pray the man enters electoral politics one day). The football bits, admittedly, are a weak point. But if you followed *Les Bleus* in 1998, you know that the football was only part of the story; it was also about the joyous, beautiful way that so many people from so many backgrounds could, briefly, transcend their differences to become united in support of a team that seemed to embody the best of a troubled country. On this vital topic, Dubois nails it. Even in a year which is crowded with football books, *Soccer Empire* stands out as one of the best. **pi**

LIFE

REMEMBERING ROBERT ENKE

DEPRESSION IN PROFESSIONAL SPORTSMEN

BOBBY BRANDON

NOVEMBER 10TH 2009

THIS WEEK THE football world was shocked by the suicide of Hannover 96 goalkeeper Robert Enke. Seemingly at the top of his career, Enke was firmly established as the first choice stopper at one of Germany's most respected clubs, and looked the favorite to be his country's number one heading into the World Cup next summer in South Africa. That was before depression claimed his life after just thirty-two years.

It is thought that Enke had never fully recovered from the shock dealt to him by the death of his two-year-old daughter, Lara, due to complications from a heart defect. I'm not a parent, so out of respect to the Enke family I won't even pretend to know that I could understand what Robert was going through: I don't.

But that's not what this piece is about.

Enke's tragic death once again brings to light the issue of depression among sportsmen. No illness is fashionable, but especially not depression, and especially not amongst men. Men are supposed to be strong and tough, capable of handling anything. This is particularly true of athletes, as Mike Messner, professor of Gender Studies at the University of Southern California in Los Angeles, explained in a fine piece written last year by the always excellent Dave Zirin: "Superman isn't supposed to get depressed."

I'm certainly not accusing Enke of falling into this trap. By all reports a quiet family man and animal rights activist, he actually seemed quite the opposite, but this is a good time to discuss a problem that faces our society everyday.

North Americans will remember last year when it was reported that Vince Young mentioned suicide before disappearing for a night, reportedly in possession of a firearm. Young and his club, the NFL's Tennessee Titans were quick to dismiss reports of depression as the media blowing things out of proportion. Whether or not Young was suffering from depression, we as a society missed an opportunity for a discussion about the illness which quietly claims many lives every year through suicide.

I'm a male, a male with depression. It took me a while to admit my problem; I didn't want to be seen as weak or feeble. Like many men, I wanted to put up a facade of strength and masculinity. Since coming to terms with my depression I've found myself to be a lot more rational, and much more stable, something which has probably saved my life. Bouts with depression can leave you feeling useless, and if you don't make your loved ones aware of what you're dealing with it becomes impossible for them to assist you, and that assistance and moral support is vital to the fragile psyche of a depressed individual.

The difficulties of admitting to depression are magnified for professional athletes in a world where bravado and hyper-masculinity can mean money, fame, endorsements and women. It becomes nearly impossible to admit to what many perceive as a weakness without realizing the courage it takes for a man to admit he has a problem.

For evidence that professional sports still has a long ways to go before claiming that it has an understanding of the disease, one has to look no further than NFL player Shawn Andrews. The Philadelphia Eagles fined Andrews $15,000 for each day of practice he missed while suffering with the illness. Though the fans and media largely supported Andrews, it still showed a glaring misunderstanding of a potentially deadly disease among our sports teams.

Bayern Munich – as polarizing a club as any – to their eternal credit seem to understand depression, and did their best to make sure that their former midfield man Sebastian Deisler was able to get help in his battle with the disease. Ultimately, recurrent depression brought an end to Deisler's career, but the awareness of the depression may have saved his life.

It's important for us to remember
Robert Enke as a husband, father,
animal lover, and fan favorite, but
we mustn't forget what claimed
his life, and we must use this as
an opportunity to wage a battle
against one of mankind's biggest
and most silent killers. **pi**

BLAME IT ON THE BOOGIE

REMEMBERING STEVEN WELLS

TOM DUNMORE

JUNE 25TH 2009

I NEVER MET Steven Wells. I always figured I would some day, but that it would be totally random – I'd be in some dive bar on a road trip to Philly to see the Fire play the new team there that he, in a small way, helped make happen, the Philadelphia Union. I presumed we'd end up shooting the shit about the Sons of Ben and Section 8 and the good fight to keep American grassroots fan culture alive in the face of the McBeast. And then we'd get into an argument about the Smiths and something would get broken and shots would be downed in excess.

Sadly, Steven Wells passed away before this could happen. He died yesterday of lymphatic cancer, at just 49-years-old. Wells made his name writing and supporting punk rock in Britain – from the Mekons to Black Flag – and

his punk rock attitude more than spilled over into his later writing on soccer in the United States. He wrote about music fiercely until the end, illustrated well by this snippet from a recent Quietus piece:

"I have argued for a long time for the state-subsidised mass-murder of all music journalists over 25-years-old. True we'd lose some cracking writers and cause a lot of human misery and suffering, but on the plus side we'd live in a universe where Q didn't exist.

"And when I say "we", of course, I mean you. Because I'd be dead.

"Frankly I think it's the only way to shut me the fuck up. I mean who gives a fuck what I think anyway? I certainly don't. And next year I'd be joined by Dom Passantino. Can I request now that we be buried togeth-er, intertwined like Ancient Greek war-rior lovers, thus causing the alien robot

squid archeologists in the year 4012 to scratch their throbbing giant computer-brain-cages with their super-advanced semi-liquid-space-metal tentacles as they wonder how these two obviously brutally murdered men – one old and the other, like, rilly rilly rilly old – were intertwined in life as they are in death?

"Or even better, every year open that grave up and sling in the next generation of 25-year-old, past-their-fucking-pontificate-date music hacks so that when the Angel Gabriel blows his horn to signal the dead to rise on the day of judgment, this huge inter-locked mass of creaking hack bones will rise from the grave like some enormous skeletal super zombie which will then engage is a mass fuck-in-a boney post-mortem sex and drugs and tediously over-told fucking anecdotes fucking orgy where slime encrusted femurs rasp chitinously into flyblown sockets and worm-gnawed fists are rammed repeatedly into crumbling pel-vic girdles. Oh fuck me I've just come all over the fucking keyboard. But it was worth it."

At times, Wells' half-crazed prose threatened to overwhelm the nuance, intelligence and truth in his arguments, but I suppose that was essential to Swells' ethos: never compromise, never limit, always excess. What marks Wells out from other 'angry' writers

was that his furious, energetic prose was just as often directed in support of something he loved as it was against the evils he hated. In this sense, he was far from a shock-jock, the coruscating nature of his writing employed for posi-tive goals.

This was why when the rest of the world was fixated on Beckham's big bucks move to the Galaxy in 2007, Wells instead introduced a British audience to grassroots American soccer fan culture, with his pieces in *Four Four Two* and the *Guardian* on Philadelphia's Sons of Ben, a supporters group for a team that then didn't exist. One of the Sons of Ben founders emphasises the importance of Swells' support:

"He wrote about us in Philadelphia Weekly, FourFourTwo, and The Guardian...apart from a small little blurb in Sports Illustrated he was the source of all our solid media credits for months. He was at our first tailgate – he took the well-known picture of all of us there. He saw what we were really doing and what we were capable of doing before any of us did, I think. He gave us relevance."

Wells' magnum opus on the SOB came last year after the announcement the city would have an MLS team in 2010, with an epic feature published in the *Philadelphia Weekly*:

"Meet the Zolos – the crazy fans of Philadelphia's yet-to-be-named American soccer club. They're better known as the Sons of Ben (SOB). They've got a club crest, flags, a Latin motto, a customized bass drum, six different scarf designs, thongs, mousepads, aprons and mugs. Lord knows how many songs and chants, and-at last count-2,010 members. (Hence Zolos. Get it?)

"They've also got bitter rivalries with Major League Soccer (MLS) teams D.C. United and New York Red Bulls. And the New England Revolution hate them too. As do fans of the Portland Timbers and Toronto. Already. Despite the fact that Philly doesn't actually have a team yet. How Philly is that?

"As you've almost certainly heard, there's a $115 million soccer-specific stadium and an MLS franchise coming to Philly. To nearby depressed-to-hell Chester, actually. They start play in 2010. (Zolo. Get it?) And the reason we're getting a team?

"You can never underestimate the passion of the fans," says Ed Rendell at a press conference in Chester. "You can't measure it. Believe me, this group's excitement and desire had a lot to do with why we're here announcing this franchise."

"Big Ed goes on to compare the SOB to the Eagles' 700 level. Which is kind of flattering to Eagles fans."

Wells' point, which he made again and again, was that the vibrant potential of grassroots soccer culture lay in its contrast to the stilted atmosphere of professional American sports at the highest level, which sees adult fans infantalised and spoonfed seemingly anything to distract them from the game itself.

Wells understood that what happened at the bottom was just as important – perhaps even more so – as what happened at the top for the future of soccer in the U.S., as he told Richard Whittall in an excellent interview at *EPL Talk*:

"The history of soccer is the US isn't just the history of the professional game. There's also the (in many respects way more interesting) history of the grassroots game. Maybe I'm being optimistic, but even if pro-soccer in the US once again shits the bed (and let's not forget that last year saw both the collapse of NFL Europe and the AFL indoor football league) I don't really think that would impact grassroots soccer.

"Just as soccer boosters tended to massively overestimate just how much the establishment of the WUSA and the arrival of Beckham would "grow"

soccer in the US, I think we also tend to worry a little too much about our failures and setbacks."

"I think grassroots soccer survives and continues to flourish in the US for a whole host of reasons, but perhaps also because it fills a previously empty evolutionary niche.

"In much of the rest of the world, you'll find soccer balls in every work space (I've never been on a British rock band tour bus without one, for instance.) First chance you get, you set up goalposts, in the parking lot maybe, and you kick off.

"The nearest US equivalent is basketball. But basketball without the hoops is futile. In soccer almost any-thing can be used as a goalpost, hell, you don't even need a ball.

"I see kids playing pick-up gridiron in parks and it seems to be spectacularly futile and unsatisfactory waste of time, with most of the players stood around doing nowt.

"And there's the American oddity of kickball. I passed a school play-ground recently and I thought: Oh my god, they're playing soccer.

"Then I thought: No they're not, they're playing kickball.

"This I found extremely odd. I'd even go as far as to say that the day that soccer really succeeds in the US isn't when the US wins the world cup, it's when it becomes the default sport in the nation's playgrounds.

"Which – in Darwinian terms – it really should, being far better suited to that arena (and way more fun as well as being better exercise) than all the alternatives. Way to go yet though…"

Cancer means that Wells will not be around to see whether this happens. His battle with the disease does leave another legacy – his brutally honest and ferocious piece on his struggle within the American healthcare system will, I hope, be read by many more.

"This is the tale of a smartarse Brit getting lost in the Philadelphia health system. The highlights – edited for shock value – include cockroaches, urine-drenched bathrooms, a crazed geriatric chip-sucker, a frenzied attempt to masturbate into a speci-men jar while the chap in the next bed watches Patton at a libido-shattering 128 decibels, and nurses hiding their name badges while my wife screams, "My husband's got cancer. Get off your arse and get him his fucking painkill-ers now!"

"The story also features Kafkaesque data chases, a scrotal sac swollen to the size of a football, glimpses of oak-paneled $300-a-night posh-patients' rooms where protein shakes come in silver salvers, the hor-ror of the catheter they stick down your cock (and this is legal, why?) and the nightmare foot-long scented candle of compacted fecal matter that was

*so hard to shift that I collapsed and
had to be given oxygen the first time
I tried.*

*"Plus more love, affection and
staggeringly efficient professionalism
from amazing doctors and incredible
nurses than you could possibly believe.
And more really, really, really great
free drugs than you could shake a
shitty stick at.*

*"Seriously, having experienced
everything from industrial-strength
stool softeners to the same anxiety
and pain relief medicine they issue to
medics in the Marine Corps, I have
to wonder why anybody in America
would ever take crappy street drugs.
Join the Army and get shot. It's got
to be cheaper in the long run, and it's
totally legal.*

*"Did I type that out loud? I'm
sorry. It's the synthetic heroin. It's
great but it does have the unfortunate
side effect of turning you into an emotional Republican."*

Wells' final piece, which he
filed last week, was one of his best
composed rants as he approached
the end. Wells' departure to punk
rock heaven leaves a big blank
space we might never fill again.
His last printed words:

I blame it on sunshine.
I blame it on the moonlight.
I blame it on the boogie. **pi**

THE EVOLUTION OF AMERICAN
SOCCER SUPPORT

THROUGH A KID AT HEART

PETER WILT

FEBRUARY 24TH 2010

I'VE OFTEN TALKED about how too many Americans expect an instantaneous soccer revolution, when in fact they should recognize that the sport has instead undergone a phenomenal, yet deliberate, *evolution* over the last twenty years.

That point was driven home to me recently in the person of long-time Chicago soccer supporter Al Hack who died suddenly Valentine's Day morning. To me, Al represents a generation of Americans who helped escort soccer from the dark ages of the sport in the 1980s to today's relatively enlightened era in which soccer plays an important and relevant part in the lives of the majority of Americans.

It was at a soccer game, of course, where I first met Al – a Chicago Storm indoor soccer match at the UIC Pavilion – four years ago. I knew Al as a Chicago Fire and Chicago Red Stars fan, but mostly I knew him as the jovial and loving father of two soccer passionate girls. One of his daughters, Nicole, was the founding leader of the Chicago Red Stars supporters' group Local 134.

Al's soccer-loving path reflects the evolution of both the size and the nature of soccer's generational movement into the American mainstream. He was a conduit of soccer's growth in the United States. Like so many other American men, he was first introduced to the sport through interaction with immigrants and an opportunity to connect with his children in a youth soccer program. Al coached his daughters

Nicole and Allie for a total of 13 years. He didn't know a lot about soccer, but he loved sports and he loved his daughters, so when the Tinley Park Bobcats needed a coach, Al stepped in.

Through soccer he was able to connect with his daughters. Before you knew it, Al was taking the girls to Chicago Power professional indoor soccer games at the Rosemont Horizon. Some of Nicole's fondest childhood memories were attending those Power games with her dad.

Al and Nicole didn't go to the games by themselves. Al worked for 33 years at the Andrew Corporation in Chicago's south suburbs. Many of his co-workers were European immigrants who brought their passion for soccer to Chicago with them. It was one of those co-workers, Jake Setter from Germany, who first introduced Al to soccer and went with him to pro soccer games...first it was Chicago Sting games, then Chicago Power games and later Chicago Fire games – at Soldier Field, Cardinal Stadium and finally Toyota Park.

Jake and Al were later joined by fellow co-worker and Scotsman Ian Brown and then by Al's former Chicago Fire ticket sales rep Nick Zahos.

Like so many other new Americans, the immigrant friends knew the sport well and were more than happy to share their knowledge – and opinions – with Al. Through long discussions and debates over many beers at many soccer matches, Al learned the sport and gained a passion for it. A passion that he passed on to his daughters. That transference of passion in sport from father to child had been occurring in American sports for more than a century...but now with Al's generation it was happening with soccer.

His daughters played throughout their youth. Allie also played some in high school and excelled in gymnastics, too. Nicole continued with soccer in high school and continues to play recreational indoor and outdoor soccer today. Al and Jake attended the World Cup at Soldier Field in 1994 and longed for the day Chicago would get an MLS team they could support.

Al used the Fire to provide a social connection for his whole family. His wife Vivian and their daughters also attended soccer matches along with Al, Jake, Ian and Nick.

"Obviously, Allie, my mom and I were also his soccer buddies," Nicole said. "He thought that soccer would keep us together as a family and I must admit it was working. The brick I bought my parents that's in front of Toyota Park says 'A red heart can never be broken', and our hearts may be hurting right now, but they will never be broken. My dad was my ultimate soccer buddy," she said.

Al became a veteran of attending soccer matches. He no longer coached, but he had gained much knowledge from his coaching, his years of watching soccer and debating it with Jake, Ian and Nick. He wasn't content just sitting quietly in the stands. He was vocal and even joined Section 8 on occasion to provide colorful support to the home team.

The last time Al and I spoke was a couple weeks ago at the Section 8 Chicago Annual General Meeting. He wasn't one of the younger attendees, but he certainly was one of the youngest at heart. Vivian told me at the wake how much he enjoyed our conversations. I can say the same, because he always was laughing and always made me feel better about whatever was going on at that time. She then provided me with great praise by telling me that my spirit reminded her of Al. Surely, no higher compliment could be paid.

After many years of supporting the Fire, a professional women's team came to Chicago. His daughters, all grown up by then, were thrilled and Al was thrilled. Again, he committed to supporting the team with Red Stars season tickets for his family.

To me, Al's life seemed to center on his family and soccer. It was only at his wake where I realized the fullness of his interests and the scope of his impact. Long lines of mourners snaked around the funeral home for more than five hours to pay tribute to this wonderful man. The lines wound past dozens of images that showed his love of Walt Disney World, the White Sox and the Eiche Turners as well as the love I already knew he had for the Fire, Red Stars and family.

While Al has passed, his wonderful memory lives on in all who were fortunate to share a beer, a cheer and a laugh. His individual legacy will live on in Vivian, Allison, Nicole and his countless friends, but he is also part of a generation whose legacy was largely unforeseen 20 years ago.

A generation that transitioned and translated a foreign sport to their kids and helped make it a part of the fabric of American culture as much as Walt Disney World and Valentine's Day.

Thank you Al and thank you to the millions of others who joined him on that successful journey. **pi**

FROM THE DAYTON DYNAMO

TO SAPRISSA STADIUM

DAVID KEYES

NOVEMBER 20ᵀᴴ 2009

THE DAYTON DYNAMO were, I now realize, far from a high-quality team. But in Southwest Ohio in the early 1990s, there were few better options. European soccer on television would come later that decade, but growing up the only live option was the Dynamo.

The Dynamo did not even play the true 11-a-side game seen around the world. Instead, they played a 5v5 indoor game more akin to hockey – walls and penalty boxes included – that was the only professional soccer in the US after the collapse of the North American Soccer League. The Dynamo played in the National Professional Soccer League, but for all I knew at the time, it was as good as the Champions League.

When MLS came along in 1996, I had learned enough about the world game to be embarrassed by my previous infatuation with the Dayton Dynamo. I had, in fact, become something of a soccer snob and held my nose at Americanizations such as having the clock count down on the scoreboard and hockey-style shootouts to break ties. But the opportunity to watch true professional outdoor soccer was enough for me to hold my nose at its silly "innovations."

I was at the first Columbus Crew game and can still recall Bo Oshonyi's long punt to Brian McBride, which the then unknown striker put away with aplomb (the American football-sized field made such a goal easier). My soccer-watching diet was getting better. The modest meal of early MLS was dramatically better than the scraps that were the NPSL, but I knew others were eating five-course meals, and I wanted at least a taste.

For that, I would have to wait until 1997. During the first half of that year, I was an exchange student in Costa Rica. Even before I left, I had circled the date on the calendar when the US would play the Ticos in a qualifier in the capital, San Jose. March 23rd 2007, come hell or high water, I would be at Saprissa Stadium.

A few weeks before the game, tickets went on sale. I had heard that demand would be fierce and so I skipped school and headed to the stadium. I arrived to find a long line that included many scalpers. As I fretted in line for several hours, a reporter for Costa Rica's largest newspaper *La Nación* approached me and asked if he could interview me. I said sure and we talked about my strong desire to see the game. I was quoted in the paper the next day saying, "I'm from Ohio and the national team never plays there" (this was before the building of Crew Stadium).

And though I have no memory of this now, I apparently also told the reporter that if I couldn't get tickets at the stadium, I would go to the American embassy to ask if they could help me (little good that would have done me). After

nearly half a day of waiting, I gave in and paid a scalper the equivalent of $70 for two tickets to the game, an astronomical mark-up of the face value. I was slightly embarrassed at having paid so much for the tickets, but at least I was going to the game!

When gameday finally arrived, I approached the Saprissa Stadium feeling proud of my special status as a ticket holder only to find that scalpers had had trouble selling their wares and tickets were going for far less than what I had paid. Ignorant gringo that I was, I didn't realize that the game was taking place during Holy Week, a period during which many Costa Ricans head out of town. The lack of demand meant that ticket prices plummeted on game day, by kick-off going for around $1 a piece.

I entered the stadium along with an exchange student friend of mine and we realized that our seats would leave us all alone in a stadium full of Costa Ricans, most of whom seemed friendly (but then, the game hadn't started yet). Seeing some other American fans across the way, we sweet-talked the stewards into letting us into that section. We may have been a small group (50 at the most), but we were excited and passionate in our support of the U.S. national team.

Pre-game was mostly filled with Costa Rican fans taunting American forward Roy Lassiter with chants of "Lassiter *ladrón*." Lassiter had played in Costa Rica for several years, during which time he had apparently not paid his taxes (*à la* Diego Maradona), a fact that the authorities reminded him of on his return to the country with the national team. Other American players were "greeted" to Costa Rica with bags of urine and batteries hurled at their heads.

The game itself is mostly a blur in my mind. I seem to recall that it was exciting, and indeed it must have been, as it finished 3-2 to the Costa Ricans. Mostly, I remember the atmosphere. It was incredible to witness the noise as the players came onto the field. The roar of the crowd was deafening and the confetti they threw on the field turned it from green to white.

Throughout the game, the entire stadium sang in unison: "*Vamos, vamos los ticos. Que esta tarde tenemos que ganar*" ("Let's go, let's go Ticos. Today we must win"). We American fans got chuckles of approval from neighboring fans when we substituted gringos for Ticos and sang along with them.

The general level of English instruction in Costa Rican schools is comically bad, but there is one word that nearly everyone in the country – or at least nearly everyone in the stadium that day – knows: sorry. Showers of "sorry, sorry, sorry" rained down on me and my fellow Americans as we left the stadium, but we had the good humor to laugh along with our taunters. We waved to fans who smiled at us as they practiced their English on us. In many ways, I think it's for the best that Costa Rica won; I'm not sure how friendly the fans would have been if they had not.

I left the stadium that March day with a lighter wallet than should have been the case, but much richer in terms of soccer experience. I saw first-hand the passion that drives fans in Costa Rica, and throughout the world. It is an infectious passion, and I was sickened that day. I have yet to recover. pi

BOOTH, FISH AND ME

PLAYING WHILE WHITE IN AFRICA

ANDREW GUEST

AUGUST 1ST 2009

You don't run into a lot of Irish folks in Africa. Lots of Canadians, Norwegians, Japanese, and Australians, but very few Irish. Maybe that helps to explain why Sport Against Racism Ireland was among the groups who, during June's Confederations Cup in South Africa, were quick to assume that predominantly black crowds were booing the lone white player on the South African national team, Matthew Booth.* In fact, the crowd was celebrating Booth by enunciating and elongating his name: "BOOOOTH." The sounds are certainly easy to confuse. But the meanings could only be confused by anyone who hasn't spent much time in Africa.

During June's Confederations Cup I was actually surprised, and I suppose pleased, by how little race

came up as a major issue. As the first African World Cup approaches, it seems as though the rightful focus is more on poverty and economic justice – the challenges and expenses of creating a massive sport spectacle when there are so many other needs raises complex questions about global inequality. But issues of race bring their own complexities, often wrapped up with issues of economic inequality, and the relationship between race and soccer is one of many interesting issues I suspect will get much attention in the run-up to World Cup 2010.

AZUNGU IN MALAWI

Beyond general intellectual curiosity, my amateur interest in race and African soccer is decidedly personal. During a two year Peace Corps stint between 1996 and 1998 I spent a season as the only white player in Malawi's 400,000 Kwacha Lifebuoy Super League. Prior to Peace Corps, I had been a decent college soccer player, and played two years in the USL (then called the "USISL") with some moderate success. But I was always a step too slow to think realistically about anything more. So when I joined Peace Corps I was mostly ready to accept the end of my playing days. But in joining Peace Corps I ended up with something of a choice between an assignment in Tonga and an assignment in Malawi, and the fact that Tongans prefer rugby helped me make my decision. In the back of my mind I hoped I might find a way to tap Africa's passion for soccer.

After settling into my work assignment at the Malawi Institute of Education I stumbled into a connection with the University Football Club (UFC), a mediocre team in the top Malawian league comprised of a mix of students and affiliates. When I approached the team with an interest in trying out, I made it a priority to try and moderate any expectations: having watched some 'Super League' games I thought I was a good enough player to contribute, but knew I was not good enough to be a star. Unfortunately, being an "Azungu" (the ubiquitous term in Malawi referring primarily to "Europeans") in Malawi almost inevitably meant confronting expectations, often having to do with wealth and ability, that arose from a challenging mix of colonialism, satellite TV, and global economics. Though such expectations are infinitely problematic and frustrating, on average they tend to be excessively generous to the Azungu. Far from experiencing derogatory racism, I suffered from people thinking too much of me.

Though I don't know much about Matthew Booth, I suspect he has also had more of people thinking too much than of people thinking too little in his experiences as a white man playing soccer in Africa. With a bit of online searching you get the idea that Booth has led a pretty interesting life: raised in Cape Town, coming of age during the end of Apartheid, working with a human rights lawyer to challenge an early contract with Cape Town Spurs (according to the career history on his own website), representing South Africa everywhere from Malawi to Georgia to Trinidad and Tobago to Burkina Faso, marrying a stunningly beautiful (black) South African model, spending the bulk of this decade in the Russian Premier League, back in South Africa for the run-up to the World Cup. I certainly suspect that the man has some good stories. But not having access to those stories, the only thing I really know is that most (though certainly not all) South African soccer fans seem to enjoy watching Matthew Booth play.

My own experience was a bit less certain. The Malawian Super League was an officially amateur affair – the type of league where all the teams are sponsored by companies (Bata Bullets were sponsored by the shoe company) or government agencies (Telecom Wanderers were sponsored by the Ministry of Post and Telecommunications) that provide cushy jobs for really talented players, and some meal money for everyone else.

It was, however, the only league in the country of any significance and had a regular place of prominence in the sports news. My UFC team was a minor club and though my appearance on their roster did garner a vague article or two about an American training for the Super League season, I mostly came as a surprise to the few hundred fans attending most of our games.

Our home field, the Zomba Community Center Ground, was a dusty brick and tin job with a few concrete benches and most the seating on a hillside. In my first few games I caused a bit of a stir – playful jibes and excited laughter met my lumbering attempts to join in the team's rhythmic warm-up runs. After kick-off, the first minutes set the tone for the rest of the day; during one or two games I held my ground defensively and made smart decisions with the ball – the hillside would come alive with cheers. More often, however, my lack of pace would get exposed and the hill would turn on me – a rollicking four beat chant of "Azungu out! Azungu out!" was more than enough to send the coach scurrying for a halftime substitution.

The team overall had more downs than ups. My Malawian teammates were good guys, but the season was frustrating for everyone and they never quite knew what to make of me. If anything, they gave me too much respect. As the frustrations mounted, it turned into a lonely time for me. Being Azungu brought curiosity and deference, but it also brought a sense of isolation that was the hardest thing about my time in Africa.

THE NEW MARK FISH?

A year later, still trying to make sense of it all, I sat down with my Malawian teammates to get their perspectives (and to try my hand at the type of field research I was planning to pursue in graduate school). I mostly asked them about their own experiences with soccer, but I also slipped in a few questions about what had happened to me. I was reminded of some of these conversations when reading about Matthew Booth. My teammates reinforced for me that among many Malawians, "People always think that, just because he is a white player, and everywhere you see that, for example, major leagues of the world are always dominated by white people...hey, we have a savior here."

The point is that in my experiences with soccer in Africa white players are much more likely to be the targets of undue admiration rather than undue derision. Though this may have been particularly true in Malawi (during a more recent stint in Angola I found much less deference to "Europeans" and a good reminder that Africa is not just one place),

I've been around enough to know race-based resentments among black Africans are much less likely to turn into personal vendettas than you might think. In my case, even when I proved something of a disappointment on the field, Malawians loved to watch me play and some even cheered me with the approving moniker "Fish!" – a reference to the South African center back Mark Fish who was his generation's Matthew Booth. Fish was a tall and flamboyant center back who made 62 appearances for his country during a career that included professional stops with Jomo Cosmos, Orlando Pirates, Lazio, Bolton Wanderers, and Charlton Athletic.

In fact, one of my favorite moments during my playing days in Malawi came nowhere near the field – riding in a car stopped at a somewhat frightening police check point when travelling through a small Malawian town an hour from my home, a group of boys playing on the side of the road recognized me and starting chanting "Fish! Fish! Fish!" The police waved me through. It may be relevant to note here that I look absolutely nothing like Mark Fish. He has the swarthy look of a Mediterranean sea captain, while I look more like a pasty Minnesota farm boy. But we were both white guys playing soccer in Africa, and for the Malawians that was close enough. It was also cause for celebration.

Of course, my own minor version of celebrity during my season in the Malawian Super League was nothing in comparison to Mark Fish in South Africa. His story, along with that of his 1998 World Cup partner in the central defense of Bafana Bafana Lucas Radebe, was framed by at least one book as the story of the new South Africa (*Madiba's Boys: The Stories of Lucas Radebe and Mark Fish*). He has also been the subject of a 2007 academic analysis by Chris Bolsmann and Andrew Parker titled *Soccer, South Africa and Celebrity Status: Mark Fish, Popular Culture and the Post-Apartheid State*.

Bolsmann and Parker argue that Fish generated an enthusiastic following in South Africa at least in part as a reaction against racism: black soccer fans appreciated Fish both for his talent and for his willingness to counter the racial norms of apartheid that artificially segregated blacks to soccer and whites to rugby and cricket. Ironically, due to his being a white soccer player Fish represented the possibility of a new South Africa

that did not depend on racial categories.

Watching the Confederations Cup from a distance it seems to me that Matthew Booth has taken up this mantle and symbolic importance. South Africa certainly struggles with issues of race and racism, as do most countries in the world, but South Africans also take well-deserved pride in the possibility of being a true "Rainbow Nation." The soccer field offers one of many symbolic spaces towards this possibility, allowing white players to be appreciated and celebrated because of how they contribute to an admirable ideal.

Of course, South Africans along with Africans of all nationalities also just appreciate good soccer. On a trip through Uganda and Kenya in the summer of 2008 I was endlessly amused by tributes to teams such as Manchester United and Chelsea in the most unlikely places.

The fishing boat painted with the Man Utd logo in rural western Uganda had little to do with race and much to do with the satellite television access to Premier League highlight packages. The shanty-town school chalkboard in Nairobi covered with homage to Frank Lampard and John Terry seemed mostly to be honoring the best talent money can buy.

This ultimate appreciation for the game itself is what finally proved my own downfall during my time in the Malawian Super League. The pace of the games was frenetic – there was much skill and quickness to admire. But the tactics were what you might expect of a country where most players learned the game on their own without access to much coaching. My robotic American style of play was a poor match, and being white just confused the matter. As one of my teammates reflected:

"People were just expecting too much, because the greatest players from Europe, America – that is how they were rating you, they were expecting that. They didn't know you. When people don't get what they are expecting, they take away.

"The mere fact that you are Azungu, I was noticing players on the other teams, when they get the ball, they want to actually dribble the Azungu so they can go back and say – Jack, I dribbled the Azungu. The feeling of most Malawians is that the Azungu is superior, so if they get to dribble an Azungu, yeah!"

Despite the confusion I persisted for months, hoping that I might adapt while my teammates and fans adjusted their expectations. But things mostly just got worse. I finally gave up on a bright November day. We were playing the Blue Eagles (sponsored by the Malawian Police) at the Lilongwe Stadium, a crumbling hulk of cement risers filled with a few hundred fans. The pitch, though among the best in the league, was pock-marked and rough.

Both teams were in the bottom half of the table, and my presence seemed to offer the only small flutter of enthusiasm among the fans and the Blue Eagles. But after a poorly timed tackle in the second half, I came up with a bloody knee that caught the eye of a Blue Eagles player. He froze briefly with a look of uncertainty. Then, with great enthusiasm, began excitedly pointing and cackling. Look everyone, the Azungu bleeds! Suddenly flesh and blood, a mere moral who can't even make a clean tackle, I somehow knew I was done.

I stuck around UFC for the rest of the season, helping out with practices and games however I could. But in retrospect I imagine the most important thing I did that season was to offer a different type of Azungu footballer to Malawians familiar primarily with Mark Fish and the EPL: the not very good Azungu. In the context of June's Confederations Cup, I offer this as a reminder that there are some white players that deserve to get booed. But Matthew Booth isn't one of them. Fortunately, African soccer fans are smart enough to figure that out on their own. **pi**

    * *The Sport Against Racism Ireland claim was described by Jere Longman in a June 27th 2009* New York Times *article ("Scrutiny for South Africa Year Before World Cup"), and notes the "group later acknowledged its mistake." It seems that several other reporters and observers made the same mistake.*

THE POLICE PLAYING THE POLICED

JENNIFER DOYLE

JUNE 11ᵀᴴ 2009

I AM A founding officer for the Union Football League, an AYSO-affiliated adult league which plays near downtown Los Angeles. When we heard that the Los Angeles Police Department (LAPD) would field a team during our first season, we were a bit wary.

The field is smack in the middle of Pico-Union, and right down the street from the new police station. This is the home of the infamous 1990s Ramparts Scandal. It is also the neighborhood of the May Day "Melee" in which the LAPD used violence to break up a peaceful march and demonstration calling for reform in immigration policies in the United States, and for recognition of the rights of the migrant communities that define the region (a video of that event includes silent footage of demonstrators being pushed at gunpoint across the soccer field). The cops in this neighborhood have long been working under a self-generated cloud of fear, anger, and mistrust.

The whole experience was something of a nightmare. The LAPD squad is muscle-bound and incredibly fit. They are a tough team. They can run you into next year, and they don't shy away from using their size advantage to win the ball. Nothing wrong with that.

But their team also has a coach who shouts from the sidelines the likes of: "Take him out out!" "Take him down!" and "Get him!" – while wearing a dark blue jacket with the letters LAPD across his back. Guys from several teams reported more disturbing remarks made on and off the field by LAPD players – e.g. "This [the game] is all you have, you have nothing to go home to."

As fit as they are, their ball handling is just OK. When confronted with the better teams in our league – who play a fast passing game dependent on great footwork, bursts of speed and an ability to change direction and turn in a blink – the cops were sometimes undone by the very thing they normally rely on: their size, and their physicality.

It's an old story: the confrontation between a militaristic defensive game and the flash, bob and weave of *joga bonito*. In general, when things didn't go their way, they got visibly and audibly frustrated, and played not better but just meaner and harder. They played with a win-at-all-costs attitude, and were convinced every whistle made in their direction was misplaced. They complained endlessly about the referees – so much so that I suspect the refs dreaded working their matches.

As I'm the league treasurer, I may have spoken with the team the most. Every week I would check with them about the league fees, make small talk and try to get to know them. I had a series of conversations with their manager about the problems that were arising around their

presence. He was genuinely upset by the tone of the games and remarkably open in sharing his perspective and experience.

It seemed to them that neither their opponents nor the referees could forget that they were the "cop team." He said that they never had this problem playing in more Anglo settings. Although the majority of the guys on the LAPD team are Latino, they seemed only to have problems playing in parts of the city like ours.

It all came to a head towards the end of the season. It was a big game between the LAPD team and Nikys Sports – an unbeatable squad sponsored by the soccer shop across from our field. Nikys has everything – skill, knowledge, experience, strength and speed. In my opinion, Nikys are capable of playing some of the best and most entertaining football you'll see in California.

I didn't get to see that the night they took on the LAPD. The referee lost control of the match after 30 minutes, and fearing that a player would be seriously hurt, or that the game would descend into a melee, he rightly called it off. I've never seen that before.

All of the referees and the spectators I spoke to held the LAPD team responsible for the disintegration of the match. Their game was marked that night by verbal abuse, dangerous and pointless tackles, and just plain rage.

The guys from Nikys, normally one of the more 'emotional' of the teams in our league, were remarkably calm about it all and went on to finish the season with an almost perfect record.

The day after that disastrous match, the manager withdrew the LAPD from the league altogether. Their departure was inevitable and we were glad they knew this. We talked on the phone, and I learned this wasn't the first time that this had happened. The manager (who had spent the weekend assisting with the Santa Barbara wildfires) sounded exhausted and depressed. It had been years since they had tried playing in a league like ours, because previous attempts had ended exactly this way. He told me, in fact, that Internal Affairs had advised them to withdraw (because they feared that if they injured an opposing player, the LAPD might be sued).

In that conversation, I caught a glimpse of the complexity of his position – and the seductive lure of the fantasy we'd all indulged in by imagining things could unfold any other way than they ultimately did.

People wax romantic about the utopic possibilities generated through football, but realities of power, authority and significant histories of abuses of both can't be wished away.

It is not possible for a cop team to play in one of the most policed neighborhoods in the region, and imagine that we can all forget who they are. The cops don't forget it. The player stopped and searched as he pulled into his own driveway ("lots of Toyotas in this neighborhood are stolen") and then issued a citation for making a dangerous turn (!) won't forget. Nor will the guy with a brother in jail. Nor the guy harassed because of his immigration status. Nor will the guy arrested last week for doing what people do at parties in the Hollywood Hills sans repercussion.

Forgetting is a form of entitlement. Forgetting who and where we are is a luxury. If Anglo teams in middle class swaths of beachside communities "forget" they are playing the cops, it's because they do not experience themselves as "policed." And if the cops can forget that they are cops when they play those teams, it's because those guys aren't the ones they are policing.

I would like to think that football is not a space of forgetting, but of remembering. Remembering who you are, and who is with you — remembering a history not with words, but in movement.

I will stop myself here, before I get romantic.

I was glad to see the cop team leave, and am happier even still to let go of the atavistic scrap of liberalism that overrode my gut feeling about the wisdom of inviting the police into our space of play. **pi**

SEXISM HURTS

JENNIFER DOYLE

MAY 14ᵀᴴ 2008

SEXISM CAN BE simple and obvious (for example, the F.A.'s effective ban on the women's game for much of the twentieth century). More often, it's subtle, complex, and really hard to tackle. Take, for example, the impact of poor medical understanding of women in general and of women athletes in particular.

We see this in the alarming frequency with which women athletes who play soccer and basketball suffer ACL tears. The ACL tear is a very serious knee injury, requiring complex surgery and a lot of recovery time.

The New York Times Sunday magazine recently published an in-depth story about young women soccer players, the injuries they sustain, and the difficulty we have in dealing with them. The article is adapted from Michael Sokolove's forthcoming book *Warrior Girls: Protecting Our Daughters Against the Injury Epidemic in Women's Sports*. (Can I just say: I hate that title. It's so paternalistic! And aimed at the parent-reader, not at the female athlete. How about – *Match Fit: Injury Prevention for Young Women Athletes?*)

This interesting article is unfortunately wrapped in a sensationalist package. Problematically, Sokolove makes news of the fact that more women are injured as more women play sports (really?!). The following rhetoric, for example, makes it seem like Title IX is the cause for the increase in 17-year-olds needing knee surgery – and as if this were in itself the problem:

"This casualty rate [JD: no statistic here, the author just means

148

the number of injuries suffered by a couple of high school teams] was not due to some random spike in South Florida. It is part of a national trend in the wake of Title IX and the explosion of sports participation among girls and young women [No soccer teams = No ACL tears]. From travel teams [these are the club teams not based in the school system] up through some of the signature programs in women's college sports, women are suffering injuries that take them off the field for weeks or seasons at a time, or sometimes forever." [Unlike men? I mean, of course women suffer career-ending injuries! At least they don't break each other's legs!]

The author then goes on to explain how girls develop differently – e.g. boys gain more muscle, but become less flexible; girls get fatter but more flexible. The author's language flirts dangerously close to naturalizing girls and women as weaker, more delicate and so on (I'm not the only one to spot this slant).

The main issue in this article, however, is women athletes' specific vulnerability to the ACL tear and the lack of understanding of the specific needs of female athletes – a failure caused not by Title IX, but by the ingrained sexism of medicine and sports culture. Towards the end of the article, the author interviews Holly Silver, a physical therapist who has developed a knee injury prevention program that should be adopted by all footballers along with their trainers.

Silver touches on some possible reasons for the high rate of ACL tears in women athletes: Girls are taught to walk and stand and move through the world differently. We curl around our chests – our bodies become shells, in a way, protecting/hiding everything 'feminine' – those bits are sources of shame, abuse, negative attention. [Ed: Found a note on *Kickster*, about the reception of the first women's game in 1894: "The *British Medical Journal* offered its professional opinion that 'we can in no way sanction the reckless exposure to violence, of organs which the common experience of women had led them in every way to protect'."]

One of the beautiful things about playing football is it forces women to free their bodies from this shell: You can't trap the ball with your chest if you are hiding it from the world. You can't make a good play if your eyes are trained on your feet. You won't have much touch or footwork if your hips are locked.

Pointing to a player with good form, Silver explains: 'She moves like a boy...Believe me, that's a good thing.'

In other words, that girl carries herself like an athlete. Girls are not encouraged to adopt this stance (knees bent, butt low to the ground). And so that posture has instead become synonymous with 'boy'. Boys, of course, aren't born moving this way – and lots of boys don't carry themselves that way (and are therefore terrorized for 'walking/throwing like a girl'). The point here is that the social inscription of gender is deep: it may be culturally produced, but it is carved into our spines, and worked into our joints. Girls need to unlearn that stuff – as athletes, they sometimes literally need to learn to walk and run.

Silver describes the extraordinary consequence of the way that girls inhabit their bodies as they play sports – if you run with poor posture, your running is not only inefficient, it harms your back, hips: all your joints, in fact. As any yoga practitioner will tell you, holding tension in your joints not only makes you less flexible and responsive (slowing your reflexes), it makes you more prone to aches and pains.

My sister coaches girls cross-country and track at Voorhees High School in New Jersey. Her teams have been very successful. Injury prevention is a big part of her program. They work on building up their strength in the gym, on minimizing strain to their muscles, on overall health and well-being. For example, she has the girls keep an eye on their iron levels – anemia is a big problem for teenage girls and young women, and can have a big impact on your development as an athlete. She's always looking for the latest information on issues like these, and keys these insights to the specifics of her sport and the people she coaches (teenage girls). Not all coaches approach their work this way.

One must recognize gender differences in order to coach/ train/treat athletes well. Those differences may be physiological, metabolic, social and psychological. For example, athletes in general are loathe to report injuries. Reporting injury or medical problems can be even harder for some girls and women.

Here are some reasons why:
»We don't want to seem weak.
In a world that reads all

physical signs of womanliness as symptoms of the weakness of your sex, getting an injury makes you feel like your body has betrayed you, again.

» Women athletes can be reluctant to own up to the differences that gender makes, because admitting to those differences has meant admitting to belonging to the 'weaker sex.' Remember: every girl – even today – will be told at some point in her life that girls can't or shouldn't play or compete. Every girl hears that girls are weak, that they aren't tough enough. Or that playing a sport makes them mannish – i.e. repugnant. To all of this, players say: Screw That, and get on with it. So, not only do we not want to seem weak – sometimes we don't want to seem like 'girls'.

» Doctors treat us differently. They don't listen to what we say about our bodies. They read everything through their ideas about our reproductive system. Our experiences with doctors tend to start off bad, and get worse. We have little reason to trust them.

» We are taught to accept certain physical symptoms as 'natural': tiredness (which is symptom number one of anemia), in particular.

» We are reluctant to talk about our bodies – sport is often the only avenue through which we get to talk about our bodies in a way that is neutral, matter-of-fact and empowering. I'll never forget listening to my sisters talk about pre-race bowel-clearing nerves and the humiliating but often hilarious situations that puts you in. As much as their stories made me laugh, I didn't really 'get' it until I started playing football and found myself at Hackney Marshes trying to act cool as we waited for the mens' teams to clear out of the damn bathrooms. Never, ever, go to Hackney, ladies, without a roll. Somehow, I associate that kind of frank and humorous talk about the body with 'jock'-culture. Some of us need encouragement to adopt this kind of attitude.

» Girls aren't always used to thinking of their bodies as something they can control. Except by starving themselves.

Add onto the above the following:

» Many girls and women play team sports on bad fields/in poor facilities.

» Ninety eight per cent of sports stores don't carry football boots made for women – and that two per cent will carry maybe two kinds. The overwhelming majority of women wear men's boots, in other words.

»Because women were prevented from playing for so long, coaching/training is modeled after the boys/mens game, and a lot of coaches are not aware of things like the frequency of ACL tears in young women footballers and the conditioning programs which might prevent those injuries.

»We accept the differences in the way that men and women move as 'natural', and so do nothing to raise girl athlete's awareness of poor posture on the field, poor running technique, the importance of being relaxed and having a good stance.

»And, most problematic of all: we don't listen to girls. We don't take their complaints seriously. We dismiss their complaints as teenage melodrama or psychosomatic weakness.

That's a lot of crap to deal with. It's why teaching/coaching/advising girls and women can be harder – but it's also why it's so absolutely rewarding. The things we learn in such settings not only change how we play – they in fact change how we live. **pi**

THE BUSINESS OF EURO 2008

MARC BAHNSEN

JUNE 30TH 2008

A S WITH ANY major international sporting event, the Big Business aspect of Euro 2008 is impossible to ignore. Setting foot in one of the designated "fan zones" seriously limits your beverage options. Looking for beer or soft drinks? Hopefully you enjoy Carlsberg beer and Coca-Cola products. Any other comparable products will not be found within the tightly controlled fan zone walls. In fact, it seems the security at the gates of the fan zones are more concerned with searching persons and their bags for outside beverages than they are interested in preventing weapons get through the gates. Seeing this causes one to question the very purpose of the so-called security.

The local food proprietors who wish to serve fans within these walls are therefore forced to oblige with UEFA's preferred choice of beverages. These overbearing corporate restrictions can make for interesting dining combinations. Any ethnic restaurant is unable to offer customers a traditional brew to match the fare – rather, a fan can only pair the available food options with the most mass produced Danish lager on the market, Carlsberg. As a beer drinker, it is easy to cringe at the lack of options but the Austrians in particular took this as a collective slap in the face to their country's rich beer heritage.

All of these restrictions and endless corporate logos covering every possible surface points to the most obvious and commanding denominator: money. UEFA is paid loads of money from top corporate sponsors to offer certain products and display exclusive advertisements within all stadia and official fan zones. "Marketing Zone" would be a more appropriate title, as UEFA pushes its own Euro 2008 product and accompanying corporate sponsored trimmings down the throat of any fan who wishes to officially participate in the marketing machine this tournament has become.

The all-encompassing corporate branding and marketing surely does not appear out of the ordinary to anyone living in today's modern society. But the shadow of Big Football Business causes one to question the authenticity of a sport that is known the world over as "The Beautiful Game". At what point can the devoted, or even casual, observer turn off the undeniable corporate presence and focus on the essence of the artistry displayed on the pitch? Or has the corporate influence already so completely dominated this sporting landscape that a willfully ignorant consumer mindstate is needed to partake in any type of modern professional football activity?

Based on the graffiti and the occasional anti-UEFA sentiment prevalent in every host city I visited (all four Swiss cities, plus Vienna), some locals undoubtedly did not appreciate this Big Football Business machine steamrolling in to their city. Sure, these cities and their residents have the opportunity to witness first hand the amazing cultural and sporting experience that comes along with being a host city. But the responsibility also allows their city squares and parks to be taken over as corporate sponsored marketing zones, not to mention trash covering every street in and around these zones, drunken football fans doing what drunken football fans do, and a chance to foot the bill of the added police and municipal presence needed to control and clean up after such a mass comes through town.

It was refreshing to see that amidst this mania fueled by UEFA imposed beer restrictions, a certain Austrian beer company seized the opportunity to play a clever counter-marketing move of their own. Ottakringer, which was founded in 1837 and is the last large brewery remaining in Vienna, changed the design of their popular Helles beer and labeled itself as the "Unofficial Fan Beer". This positioning can be seen in their current advertisements and Ottakringer even went as far as making scarves donning the particular slogan, "*Inoffizielles Fanbier*".

A Viennese man passionately insisted that his friend was not allowed in to the official fan zone because he was sporting the aforementioned Ottakringer scarf. Whether the story can be validated or exists simply as an anti-UEFA urban myth, one thing is for certain: with the hyper strict marketing machine driving the Big Business Football world we live in, this type of scenario is unfortunately not outside the realm of mere imagination. **pi**

ACTIVISM

PUTTING THE TRUST INTO FOOTBALL

AN EXAMINATION OF SUPPORTER OWNERSHIP

GARY ANDREWS

MARCH 8TH 2010

SLOWLY, A BEHIND-THE-SCENES foot-balling revolution is growing. Whether it's Portsmouth's ongoing demise, the Glazers burdening Manchester United with hundreds of millions of pounds worth of debt, Ashley at Newcastle or, lower down, the Vaughan family taking Chester City to the wall, the spotlight has well and truly turned on the owners. And with fans becoming more alarmed at the mismanagement of their clubs at boardroom level, supporters are asking whether it's time that the fans took control of their clubs.

Fan ownership, on the surface, seems sensible and logical. These are people who, unlike, say, the Glazers, have the best interest of their club at heart and care passionately about keeping their team alive and successful. Barcelona are often cited as the ideal for any fan-owned club to aim for, while other Europhiles will point to the Bundesliga's ownership model, where fifty one per cent of the club is owned by supporters.

If only it were that simple. Barcelona's ownership is a unique mix of football, politics and cultural identity, while the Bundesliga has regulation in place securing the fans' shareholding, and even then this isn't as clear cut as it sounds. English football operates on very different lines, where the free market reigns. The conditions are quite distinct.

Then there are the clubs who have already been owned by their supporters. Exeter City, the leading light in the Trust movement, is adjusting to a higher level, Brentford has moved towards a hybrid model, while AFC Wimbledon face serious choices should they get promotion to the league. Then there's Notts County and Stockport County, two teams where Trusts have tried and failed.

But with Manchester United and Liverpool fans, along with others, pushing for more fan involvement at boardroom level, it's time to ask if supporter ownership really is the way forward, or whether English football is doomed to stick with the sugar daddy model. Over the course of the week, we'll be examining the concept of Trusts, fan ownership and looking where the ownership model should go next.

THE BIRTH OF A MOVEMENT

Each Trust is different, and each was born in a different way. In Exeter City's case, it was a group of fans who wanted to club together to raise enough money to buy the striker Gary Alexander. For Brentford, it was due to concern over the possibility of losing their ground, Griffin Park, to developers. Newcastle United's Trust came from their Supporters Club as they looked to find an organised body to represent the interests of the fans. In AFC Wimbledon's case, their club had been moved to Milton Keynes and, in many

supporters' eyes, simply ceased to exist. And so on.

But there's a fundamental principle behind the Trust movement: that supporter ownership is a good thing, whether this is representation at boardroom level or outright ownership. For Brian Burgess, former vice-chairman of Brentford and recent electee to the board of Supporters' Direct, this is a principle that was picked up at an early age.

His involvement was triggered by an incident back in 1967, when Jack Dunnet, the then Brentford owner, attempted to sell the club to QPR and put the Bees out of business. "There was uproar among supporters and public meetings. I was too young to go to these but there was always talk in the newspapers that this was wrong – an individual selling the club – it's our club and the supporters should own it.

"The club was sold to a consortium of businessmen, who saved it, but I remembered that idea – the idea that supporters should own the club and it shouldn't be up for sale."

Nearly 35 years later Burgess joined the newly-formed Brentford Supporters Trust, Bees United, seeing it as an opportunity to realise that dream and in 2006

Bees United took control of Brentford. They are still the majority shareholder, although they have entered into a hybrid model with a wealthy supporter as they look to build a new stadium.

Brentford are still a rarity, though, and currently sit in League One, along with Exeter City, a completely Trust run club. After that, you have to look to non-League to find other supporter-owned clubs, such as AFC Wimbledon, Telford United and FC United of Manchester.

GOING TO THE TOP

But this certainly doesn't mean that Trusts can't play a huge part at a higher level of the game. Since the media started turning their attentions to the Glazer buyout of Manchester United and the £716 million debt they've saddled the club with, the Manchester United Supporters' Trust (MUST) have emerged as key players in both the spread of the Green and Gold campaign and the movement for fan ownership.

If this seems like a pipe dream, last week the Red Knights, a group of wealthy Manchester United fans, met to discuss a possible takeover of the club from the Glazers. It was no coincidence that a key part of this statement was a call to United supporters worldwide to support them. And this involved working closely with MUST.

Duncan Drasdo, the Chief Executive of MUST, called the Red Knights launch "hugely welcome" and in a joint statement said: "Initially the Red Knight Group has effectively set a challenge to Manchester United supporters to demonstrate they wish to see an alternative ownership proposal developed. In the first instance supporters are being asked to do this simply by joining the free online membership of the Supporters' Trust (MUST) and swelling its ranks to an initial target of at least 100,000."

To put this into perspective, Exeter City, currently the most successful Trust-run club, has just over 3,000 members. Even when there is no apparent urgency for fans to band together for their club, the Trust movement is often working behind the scenes both with the club and as a watchdog on the boardroom. Arsenal and Tottenham Hotspur may be bitter rivals on the pitch, yet off it the aims of their Trusts are remarkably similar.

For Arsenal, this can be summed up in three words:

Ownership, representation and influence. The mission statement may be wordier at Spurs, but the ideals are still the same – an ongoing positive dialogue between fans and the board, supporter representation at board level, and contributing to the future success of Tottenham.

The Arsenal Supporters' Trust formed in 2003 and Vic Crescit, a long-time member, thinks recent events at Ashburton Grove have vindicated the decision to form a Trust. "The Trust was proved absolutely right in setting up when it did. In recent years we have seen the ownership of the club transformed. Stan Kroenke, the owner of the MLS's Colorado Rapids, is now the single biggest shareholder, behind him is the Russian-Uzbek Alisher Usmanov on just over 26%.

"Then comes Danny Fiszman on 16% and Lady Nina Bracewell-Smith on 15.9%. They account for around 88% of the shares between them. Around 11% is in the hands of small shareholders like me. Around 1% of the shares are "orphan" shares where the owners have died before selling them or passing them on or can't be traced.

"The Trust owns a small number of shares held mutually in trust for its members, plus it groups together all the shares owned personally by members. By combining in this way AST has a far bigger influence in the club than the small shareholders would operating on their own in isolation."

Although the formation of the Trust was initially viewed with suspicion at Arsenal, after the board came in for criticism over the financing of the Emirates, they opened a dialogue with the Trust and the relationship has been good since, although the Trust continues to keep a close eye on boardroom developments.

THE CHALLENGES OF ANSWERING TO FANS

Although each Trust has different aims – ranging from outright ownership to simply fostering better links between fans and the club – all have a commitment to an open and democratic relationship with the supporters. There are regular elections for members to hold the Trust board to account. It is, in essence, how any democracy should work.

Offering help and guidance is Supporters Direct, an organisation that came out of the government's football taskforce report in 1999.

They may be just over ten years old, but SD have done as much to instigate fan ownership as anybody. Committed to a greater level of fan ownership, democracy and general accountability in football, and other sports, they have steadily grown in influence offering advice on everything from governance and ownership to finances. Accreditation from Supporters Direct is a sign a Trust is to be taken seriously.

But more than this, the organisation is putting serious pressure on the authorities for a more sustainable model. As their CEO Dave Boyle says: "In football's version of the tortoise and the hare, the hare wins the race and it's only two years later that the hare's house is repossessed by the bank for the loans taken out to get bionic implants, which is scant consolation for the tortoise who was sacked halfway through the race. Or, as an economist might put it, all the incentives are in the wrong place."

But while there is still a serious imbalance in football, Boyle sees plenty of progress over the past decade. "Thanks to the work of AFC Wimbledon, AFC Telford, FC United of Manchester and Scarborough Athletic, the idea that the worst thing that can happen to a club is that it be liquidated isn't as strong as it was. Fans would be told of this horrible prospect of the club disappearing and then accept whatever sharp practice, ground sale, asset strip was put forward as the least worst option. Even if that didn't happen, they'd fundraise like crazy trying to keep the club afloat when their money and energy were never going to do the job.

"But thanks to those trusts and those clubs, we know in fact what people always knew in their heart of hearts – that football in a given community isn't about the limited company formed to play it in an organised football league. If that company were to be liquidated, football would survive in the community.

"And, thanks to the success enjoyed by those clubs and the enjoyment their fans have in owning their own team, we see a lot of people being very sanguine indeed about keeping a busted flush of a small town team alive. In a nutshell, the worst that could happen used to be liquidation; now people understand that liquidation can be a cause for rebirth as a new, better type of club."

There is no better place to illustrate this than the recent goings on at Chester City, but many other clubs have seen that rebirth can be a positive thing, to say nothing of those fans who've taken the initiative and have not only saved their club but made a better fist of it than previous owners. As Boyle says: "There were people who aren't in favour of this approach to the game, who said at the start that it shouldn't happen, and couldn't happen.

"But that notion – that fans are too stupid/ignorant/passionate to be involved is a hard one to make in public, so they'd said instead that it was a lovely idea, but ultimately unworkable. Thanks to the work of the trust up and down the country, that's not an argument borne out by the evidence."

Owning a club, though, comes with its own issues, not least managing fan expectations. Exeter City is a prime example of this – the club was taken over by the Trust in 2003 after their relegation from the football league following the disastrous reign of convicted fraudster John Russell. Since then they've stabilised and have won two promotions over the last two seasons.

The club may now be struggling down the wrong end of League One, but for vice-chairman Julian Tagg, a long-time Trust member who has served on the board since the takeover, the pressure on the board is nothing new.

"There's always been a pressure," he says, "and that hasn't changed. The pressure comes from the Trust ethos of running the club and the demands of our membership, as well as the situation of the club. We've got to be creative in our approach – we can't just employ extra people.

"There's also the question of can we find a way to become competitive. We're at a level now where there really is no blueprint for how we do things."

But it's not just the challenge of League One that Tagg and the Exeter City board have to deal with – it's also having over 3,000 members, all of whom have an opinion on how the club should be run.

"The club and Trust rolls into one," says Tagg. "The Trust directors own the club and they, in turn, are bound to the membership, so we're always going to be dynamic in how we approach the club and how we want to protect the club.

"What we're really trying to do is to find a balance between being an operator and a professional club. How we look after these people [the Trust membership] is so precious. That's why we started in the first place and now the club isn't in trouble, we have to make sure of its future."

Brian Burgess has experienced similar issues with Brentford and says much of it is down to making clear the different responsibilities of the Trust and of the club board. Even then, there is still the question of where the line between the Trust and club does indeed come in.

Burgess says: "We had to say: 'Look, if the performances on the pitch are bad, if the manager needs to be changed, that's the job of the football club not the Bees United board.' But, of course, as the majority shareholder, you're interested in the company being run properly, so you're going to try and want to influence the football club board to do the right thing. And there's always been a tension in there and a learning curve about how you manage that relationship. To what extent is it arm's length, to what extent is it right to exert influence, what's the best way to assert your influence?

"I think it comes down to individuals. If you're got good individuals that people trust and they're open, as far as they can be in terms of confidentiality, then it's a lot easier. When things are going well, it's a lot easier. When things go badly then there's criticism and that's when it's really difficult.

"We appoint people and let them get on with the job. If they do a good job, that's great, if they don't, ultimately, we sack them. That's how it is – in any business, although it's more short term than any other, I guess."

WHERE DO WE GO FROM HERE?

The whole idea of Trusts and fan ownership is hugely complex. As Tagg says, there is currently no blueprint for a fan run club in League One, let alone the Premier League. And while eyes are cast at Barcelona and the Bundesliga, English football comes with its own unique set of challenges for supporters who want to run their club.

Over the rest of this series, we'll be looking at the successes and failures of the Trust movement, as well as the challenges that lie ahead, the foreign models and in-depth interviews with some of those closely involved with the movement.

But one thing, above all, that is striking about the Trust movement is the ability of fans to put aside their differences and work together for the good of the club; the idea that clubs should belong in the hands of supporters, not money men. It's an idea that would have been laughed out of town ten, perhaps even five, years ago.

As Andy Walsh from FC United of Manchester said at a recent "Beyond The Debt" rally, rivalries between supporters of football clubs are an artificial construct that mask the true enemies of football supporters – the people that run the game itself.

Or, as Crescit puts it somewhat more succinctly: "I don't ever want my football club to become a rich man's train set nor get rich quick scam. We've all seen what happens when we allow the financial tail to wag the productive dog in the world economy." **pi**

SUPPORTER OWNERSHIP

THE REALITY OF A FAN-RUN CLUB

GARY ANDREWS

MARCH 12ᵀᴴ 2010

IF PART OF a successful football club is down to luck that the right people inhabit the board-room, then Brentford can feel luckier than most that Brian Burgess decided to get involved with their supporters' trust, Bees United. It may have not always been plain sailing for the Bees since the Trust took over but, for the time being, the club's future and ground is assured. Pitch Invasion caught up with Brian at Griffin Park following his recent election to the Supporters Direct board.

There's a nice anecdote that gives you a clue to Brian Burgess' way of viewing the boardroom at Brentford. Soon after Bees United assumed control of Brentford in 2006, a friend of the family congratulated him on taking over as vice-chairman. "You own your football club!" she said, excitedly. "No," he corrected her. "The fans own my football club."

I remind Brian of this as we settle into the directors' bar at Griffin Park, Brentford's current home. Typically, rather than reminisce about the takeover, he uses it to illustrate why the fans are so important in the running of Brentford.

"That's right," he nods. "The club members vote on issues. There's a good example of that this summer. Because of the financial costs of competing in League One and the teams we have to compete with this season – the Leeds and the Charltons – the club needed a lot more cash and we couldn't really borrow any more. The club has borrowed up to its limit. The debts are secured against the value of Griffin Park.

"It really needed a cash injection which the Supporters' Trust just doesn't have and cannot provide. A deal was done by Bees United with a very wealthy supporter called Matthew Benham who had already lent us significant sums of money to refinance our previous debts. I think he'd refinanced around four million pounds worth of debt, which is interest free, he took out a loan from Barclays that was two million pounds, for example. So, instead of paying interest on that two million we have that interest free, which has been a huge boost to the club's operating expenditure.

"But that wasn't enough so he's agreed to put more money in as preference shares. He's agreed to put in a million pounds a year for the next five years. During that period Bees United will retain the majority shareholding. At the end of it there are options, so there are three possible outcomes of what could happen at the end of the five years.

"For five years at least the situation is stable, it's stable financially, it's stable in terms of the ownership model because Bees United will be the majority shareholder.

"No one was able to sign that deal until we'd had a vote of the members, so all 1,700 voting members had a say in that and 1,200 of them voted in it, which is around 70%".

That's a pretty impressive level of engagement, I say, given the apathy and disinterest many fans have in the off-the-pitch actions, let alone the idea of voting.

"Yes, and 99% of them voted in favour of the deal," he says. "But the point is it was the fans, those members, who were in control of the situation. If they didn't want to take this money from the wealthy supporter, if they didn't want that deal, they could have voted it down. The point is, the club can't be sold now without the approval of the members."

Burgess may have now relinquished his vice-chairmanship but he still remains a key part of Bees United and recently was elected to the board of the nationwide organisation Supporters Direct. Indeed, his interest in fan ownership started back in 1967, when he was a young Bees supporter growing up in Hounslow.

At the time Brentford's owner was Jack Dunnett, a Labour MP for Nottingham, who decided he'd rather own Notts County than the Bees, and decided the best way to dispose of the club was to sell it to QPR. Brentford FC would have ceased to exist.

Although Burgess was too young to get involved in the campaign to save Brentford, the idea that supporters should own their club stuck with him and was the driving force behind him signing up to Bees United in 2001 when the club was, yet again, going through one of their regular periods of financial crisis and losing Griffin Park was a real possibility.

Burgess was living and working in the Midlands at the time and getting heavily involved wasn't practical, but he soon moved into a consultancy role and returned to London. At the same time, Bees United was looking at possible plans for a new stadium.

With a background in engineering, Burgess thought he could help and stood for election to the Trust board. Within a year, he'd been elected chairman.

At that time, there was an option agreement with Ron Noades, the majority shareholder, to buy the club for two pounds providing the Trust also relieved Noades of the bank guarantees he'd used to fund the club, which totaled around four million.

After several years of raising the cash needed to buy the club off Noades, the Trust finally took

control on January 20th 2006. Burgess took the role of vice-chairman after tracking down former BBC Director General Greg Dyke, a Brentford and Manchester United fan who'd been on the board at Old Trafford, and persuaded him to take over as chairman.

All the time, though, the Trust had their eye on a new stadium. Often when new owners come in and talk about a new ground, it's cause for eye-rolling. But in Brentford's case, it's acutely needed.

"All the time the long-term strategy was to try and develop the new stadium because we knew we'd never really be sustainable as a business here at Griffin Park. We budget to lose around half a million pounds a year in order to give us even a reasonable playing budget, let alone one that can compete in League One. There are no commercial facilities here, nothing.

"It's very difficult for us to earn any kind of serious revenue because there are no corporate boxes, no hospitality suites. During the week we don't have conferencing and banqueting facilities that would enable us to make commercial revenue. It's always been the plan to build a new stadium. I've been working on it all the way through and at the end of 2007 we did a deal with Barratts to buy this site at Lionel Road and it was obvious then it would become a full-time job.

"We formed a new subsidiary called Brentford FC Lionel Road Limited just to focus on the stadium and that subsidiary, 99% of the shares are held by Brentford FC and the other 1% is a golden share for Bees United so that the site can't be developed for anything else without Bees United's approval. The idea of that golden share is to give Bees United a veto over that project being scuppered in years to come by the property developer – it's got to be used as a stadium."

But a mixture of the recession, a crash in the housing market affecting the new stadium – "Having got so close, it's desperately disappointing the external economic environment has put a hold on it" – and bad manager choices took their toll on the Bees and held up the stadium, which is where the Matthew Benham deal comes in.

"We started on a high and it went downhill quite seriously for a couple of years – it just shows the importance of having a manager who can spend your budget wisely. I think if you've got a good manager you've got to give him a budget that's good enough to compete – no one can work miracles without a sufficient budget. But beyond that, throwing an ever bigger budget at the playing squad doesn't bring you success unless the manager is really good, so you need both.

"You need the manager and you need a sufficient budget and we had neither for a couple of seasons. Since we've got Andy Scott, Andy obviously has done a really good job with a limited budget, got us up as Champions last year.

"Now the standard's higher, we're playing against bigger clubs like Leeds, Norwich, Southampton and Charlton and you need more money. Bees United couldn't raise the kind of money we needed to compete. If we had serious aspirations to get promoted from this league into the Championship you need the Matthew Benham deal, we needed that extra million pounds a year."

Although the Benham deal creates a Trust-single owner hybrid, Burgess is adamant this is the best deal for the Bees and can see other clubs following suit. "I think it's quite a good model for other Trusts because we have to live in the real world.

The economics of football as such mean it's very difficult to compete under the current regime with the big clubs and clubs who've got wealthy supporters putting in loads of money. So you need to do this sort of deal and at least we've got some safeguards in with the golden share particularly."

One area where Burgess will readily hold his hands up to getting it wrong is in his choice of managers. After Martin Allen left in 2006, Brentford went through three managers in just one season, when Leroy Rosenior, Scott Fitzgerald and Terry Butcher all took the hotseat as the Bees struggled at the wrong end of the table and eventually went down to League Two.

"We didn't have anyone on the board, including me, who really had a clue on how to pick a good football manager. It's such a big decision. If I had to say 'what is the one single most important decision a football club board has to take', it's the choice of the manager. And obviously we got it wrong three times.

"The fourth time we got it right! We could have appointed Andy Scott the first time and avoided three disasters and two years of relegation. Had we got Andy Scott first time round,

perhaps we'd have been if not in the Championship, at least pressing for it now. So it set us back a couple of years."

Burgess is not fond of the culture that calls for managerial sackings every ten minutes but recognises this is part of supporter expectations.

"I think in general, there won't be a majority of supporters who would support taking a long-term view and saying that it's much better that the club survives even if it has to go down to the Conference, rebuild and come back up again – it's actually much better to be sustainable and running sensibly, than it is to try and get lots of money from somewhere and push for success.

"Trust members might take the long-term view. Not all of them though – I think even some of them would want to take the short-term view. But you're always going to be under pressure to get short-term results, not to accept relegation as part of a longer-term strategy. So the short-term aspirations of supporters' for success is always a limiting factor, I think, in terms of how sustainably you can run the club."

Unsurprisingly, Burgess also calls owners who throw vast sums of money at clubs "unsustainable" but also recognises that as long as this continues, smaller clubs are limited as to how far they can compete. He is also a mixture of realistic and optimistic as to how far Supporters' Trusts can go.

"One glib answer is it can go as far as Barcelona and Real Madrid because they're owned by their fans, so in a way there's no limit. However, you have to look at where you're starting from and the days where Wimbledon came into the league and were able to rise up into the Premier League and win the FA Cup – in those days anything was possible. And it could be lovely to see AFC Wimbledon do that again.

"But for clubs like us with legacy and debt that we've got and the legacy of people on the board who are there not because they believe in the Trust model but because they put money into the club previously and are entitled to a seat on the board you've got that legacy that holds you back from fully exploiting the trust model.

"The biggest issue is finance – just how do you finance a competitive playing budget when you haven't got access to non-football income of one kind or another, whether it's generated by a new stadium with lots of revenue earning facilities, or whether it's

sponsorship or TV money or just soft loans or equity from wealthy individuals? I think the best hope for the Supporters' Trust movement is if the regulatory regime changes.

"I was very interested to read Lord Mawhinny's speech recently saying that things had to change, the distribution of wealth, the totally unequal distribution of wealth between the big clubs and the smaller clubs couldn't really continue, something had to be done to try and even it up otherwise too many of the smaller clubs would go to the wall."

But for all the talk of what Supporters' Trusts can achieve, Burgess is quick to point to a very specific legacy of Bees United: putting a roof on the Ealing Terrace, a project that had been talked about to Brentford for around 20 years, and one the Trust-owned club managed in two. It was, as Burgess puts it, physical evidence that the club was progressing.

Even so, the new stadium at Lionel Road remains a key part of Brentford's future and one Burgess sees as the key if the club is to progress. "I don't accept that there's any limit as long as we get a new stadium. I've always accepted we'll never really succeed above League One if we stay at Griffin Park.

"I first got involved to help out on the new stadium, and that's always been part of this. It was a strategy when we took over, it's the strategy now, I don't really see any alternative to having a new stadium on a new site, which generates a lot more income back on match days and non-match days. But if we get that then I think, well I'd like to think, we can create another Barcelona. I don't see that we have to limit our ambition.

"It will take time, maybe generations, but as long as we're financially sustainable in a new stadium with non-football revenue generating facilities, I think it can be done."

As we're leaving, Brian insists on taking me to his office so I can get an aerial view of the new stadium. It's gloomy but the shape of the area that needs developing can be just about made out. Will it have the same intimacy as Griffin Park, I wonder, a stadium where the fans are close to the pitch creating a cathedral of noise? Absolutely, he assures me. This intimacy was one of the top demands Brentford fans put on a new ground. Lionel Road, he says, will not be another identikit stadium.

At Brian's urging, I walk a different route back to the train station, past the proposed Lionel Road development. What currently resides there is a mixture of waste and industrial land. It is not particularly attractive to look at but it's easy to see how this could be transformed into something far more useful. It is, perhaps, an apt metaphor for the Trust movement as a whole. **pi**

SUPPORTER OWNERSHIP

THE SUCCESSES OF THE TRUST MOVEMENT

GARY ANDREWS

MARCH 9TH 2010

Go TO AN Exeter City away game and chances are you'll hear Grecians fans singing "We own our football club" to the home support. It's a powerful reminder of just how close the bond is between supporters and their club as City fans revel in their status as one of the few supporter-owned clubs in the country, and as one of the most successful.

The Devon club may have become an unintentional poster child for the Supporters' Trust movement but, as their vice-chairman Julian Tagg noted yesterday, there is no blueprint for a fan-run club at their current level of League One, far less the Premier League. It is an issue The Red Knights will no doubt be picking over, along with any other top-flight or Championship Supporters' Trust that harbours ambitions of owning their own club.

EXETER CITY: THE POSTER CHILD

Whenever the example of Supporters' Trusts come up, Exeter City are the obvious place to start. The Devon side may only occasionally trouble the back pages of national newspapers, but they're also the leading example of a successful Trust.

Created, initially, to find funds to buy striker Gary Alexander, the Trust, like so many others, came into its own when the club was at its lowest ebb. In the spring of 2003, Exeter had been relegated out of the Football League and were staring oblivion in the face. Their chair and vice-chair, John Russell and Mike Lewis, had just been arrested for fraud (Russell was later convicted and jailed for this), the debts were mounting and saviours were in short supply.

The Trust were invited to take over the day-to-day running of the club and embarked on a period of intensive fire-fighting. They managed to negotiate the purchase of shares from former chair Ivor Doble at the 11th hour, meaning the fans were truly in charge of the club. Had this not been completed, the Trust had a press release drawn up saying they could no longer continue to fund City and the 100-year-old club would have, most likely, been liquidated.

But while Trust members were happy to raise large sums of money, which saved the club in the long-term, much of their current success can be put down to luck or, more specifically, the moment Tony Cascarino drew them away to Manchester United in the 3rd round of the FA Cup. The money from this, and the replay, generated around £1 million, enough to pay off a large chunk of Exeter's debts. From there the club has gone from strength to strength. After losing the Conference playoff final in 2007, they went one better the following year before securing

back-to-back promotions as runners up in League Two. Heady times indeed.

Off the pitch the Trust was slowly evolving as well, from firefighters into a more professional outfit. Exeter fans with experience in the city were brought onto the board, while Denise Watts, a single mum, took over as chair of first the Trust, then the club. This was the ethos of the Trust in a nutshell – any fan could join, stand for election and find themselves shaping Exeter's future. But promotion to a higher level brought a new set of challenges. "At the moment we're the second smallest club in the division in terms of the number of people our ground can take," says Julian Tagg, the club's vice-chair and one of the original Trust members who pitched in at boardroom level in 2003.

"We look at the rugby club [Exeter Chiefs]. They've boosted attendances and, via that and their facilities, leisure dollars spent at the ground. This is something, with the current stadium, we can't quite match. There's a lot of work to be done now in how we structure the club and how we maintain that Trust ethos, and how we rebuild the stadium to bring in new finance to the club."

The stadium issue is one of the most pressing concerns for Exeter at the moment. Their Old Grandstand is on its last legs and badly needs replacing, the uncovered away terrace needs work and the whole pitch needs moving and relaying before any of this work can be done. The Grecians are reasonably fortunate in that while they don't own their ground, the local council leases it, meaning development, while slow, is possible.

For the time being, though, the club's attention is also taken up by Exeter's relegation battle at the foot of League One and while Tagg is confident they can survive, he knows their success on the pitch is tied into major off the pitch activity.

"We can compete in this league," he says, "and we may even get into the league above, all things being equal. My ambition is always to look at Crewe as an example to emulate – much of their success has been down to youth.

"If we can complete our stadium then we can sit down and think about how we go from there, but we can't do this overnight. Everybody wants instant success – that's what causes their downfall – and as long as people can be patient, we can get there but we have to do it gradually.

"We sold four young players and it took ten years of work on them before it came to fruition. That's not short-term at all. If we start with them at eight, nine, ten, who knows what could happen."

It's something that has been borne out by the club's most recent accounts, when they announced losses of £227,000 between June 2008 and May 2009, although taking into account depreciation, the trading deficit stands at £67,092. This includes the sale of youngster George Friend to Wolves for around £350,000. Since then two more youth graduates have departed – Dean Moxey for Derby and Danny Seaborne to Southampton, both for six-figure sums.

Strangely, the club would have been better, financially speaking, to have avoided promotion. The Grecians earned just £10,000 from finishing second in League Two. With bonus payments this meant Exeter would have been better off reaching the playoffs or missing out on promotion all together.

The club's debts stand at £1.8 million, although much of this is soft loans from the Supporters' Trust. Even so, this shows what a hard job a sensibly run supporter-owned club has in the lower leagues. Not that Tagg would ever consider selling up.

"An offer to buy the club would be something the members would have to vote on, and you never say never, but to me the only reason we'd do this is if we've failed and I've not got involved to preside over that. We'll do the best we possibly can.

"If someone were to come along and they were genuinely philanthropic and loved the club then we may consider this, but I'd prefer that we stayed in the hands of the supporters."

THE NEW CLUBS

Further down the chain comes two very unique success stories: AFC Wimbledon and FC United of Manchester. Both these clubs were formed out of protest – the Dons from the football league's decision to relocate the original Wimbledon to Milton Keynes, while FCUM was a reaction to the Glazers' takeover of Manchester United and a desire for United supporters to get back to their roots and ensure that ordinary supporters weren't priced out of watching their team.

Both have enjoyed impressive rises through the non-League pyramid. Since their formation in 2002, AFC Wimbledon have risen from the Combined Counties League to the Blue Square Premier, including back-to-back promotions in recent seasons, and are currently still in the hunt for a play-off spot. Similarly, FC United won promotion three times in their first three seasons before stalling at the Unibond Premier.

It is, perhaps, no coincidence that both Wimbledon and FC United have enjoyed success at lower league levels. They both started with a blank slate – there was no burden of history or, indeed, historic debts and both had a ready made community and Trust ethos in place. What's more, the crowds they were attracting gave them a significant financial advantage when competing in the lower leagues, where income is often scarce.

In many respects, both these clubs can be seen as being the purest and most successful wholly Trust-owned teams (even Exeter City have other minor non-fan shareholders) but as both teams climb the leagues and compete at a higher level, new problems arise. Just as the blank canvas benefitted these clubs at the start, so it also means each promotion is a further step into the unknown.

Chief among these issues is the now-common theme of the stadium. AFC Wimbledon currently groundshare with Kingstonian, although the Dons actually own Kingsmeadow Stadium, while FC United are tenants at Bury's Gigg Lane. But as the Dons rise up the league, the looming question is whether they continue at Kingsmeadow or look to build a new stadium in the borough of Merton, their spiritual home.

This ties in with the debate about how best for the club to progress as a whole. Gone are the days when the old Wimbledon could rise from non-League to the top flight and win the FA Cup, but if AFC have aspirations to continue their climb up the football pyramid, there will be a level, as Exeter and Brentford have found, where Trust money can only fund so far. For the time being, though, Dons fans are enjoying their status in the Conference.

FC United are a slightly different case as they have no 'spiritual' home (unless you count Old Trafford) but are well aware that their own stadium is key to future progression. Currently rental on Gigg Lane is around £5,000 per match.

The Rebels have recently submitted plans for a 4,000

capacity stadium to a supportive Manchester City Council (unlike Merton Borough Council, who are lukewarm on a Dons return) and will be looking to the end of their lease at Bury in 2011 as a rough timescale. A ground of their own will give them greater opportunity for matchday and non-matchday revenue.

What FCUM and AFC Wimbledon both have, though, that many clubs can't buy is a stable well-run board and a genuine sense of community and belonging to the club. And in non-League, where many sides are an unexpected bill away from crisis, that counts for a lot.

THE PHOENIX FROM THE FLAMES

As Dave Lister once said to the hologram Rimmer in Red Dwarf: "Cheer up, death isn't what it used to be," and that could equally apply to football clubs teetering on the brink today. If your club went out of business years ago, that was the end – or if a new club was set up with the same name, it would take decades to get back to where you once were, as Aldershot and Accrington Stanley can testify.

But if a club collapses financially today, there is light at the end of the tunnel and often the Supporters' Trust is waiting in the wings to reform the club and put it on a more even keel, giving fans the opportunity to run their club as opposed to an owner with big promises but smaller pockets.

Dave Boyle, the CEO of Supporters Direct, is one of those who urges fans not to despair if it looks as if their club is going to the wall. "The idea that the worse thing that can happen to a club is that it be liquidated isn't as strong as it was," he says.

"Fans would be told of this horrible prospect of the club disappearing and then accept whatever sharp practice, ground sale, asset strip was put forward as the least worst option. Even if that didn't happen, they'd fund-raise like crazy trying to keep the club afloat when their money and energy were never going to do the job.

"But thanks to those trusts and those clubs, we know in fact what people always knew in their heart of hearts – that football in a given community isn't about the limited company formed to play it in an organised football league. If that company were to be liqui-dated, football would survive in the community. And, thanks to the success enjoyed by those clubs

and the enjoyment their fans have in owning their own team, we see a lot of people being very sanguine indeed about keeping a busted flush of a small town team alive."

Perhaps the leading example of this is AFC Telford, who were formed out of the ashes of Conference side Telford United. The Bucks were liquidated in 2004 when the chairman and owner, Andrew Shaw, got into business difficulties and had to put his entire empire into administration. But no sooner had United ceased to exist, the Trust was waiting in the wings to create the phoenix club.

Having secured use of Telford United's New Bucks Head ground, the club was placed in the Northern League Division One. Within three years they were playing in the Conference North, with crowds averaging around 2,000. Far from killing the support for football in the town, Telford United's demise actually re-ener-gised support. The town rallied round and created a community club that was far more engaged with its supporters. In both poten-tial and execution, AFC Telford are the best possible advert for a supporter-owned phoenix club.

Scarborough Athletic are another example of the supporters

rallying to keep professional football in the town after the original
club, Scarborough FC, went bust
in 2007 with debts of £2.5 million. Again, a new club rose from
the ashes under the management
of the Supporters' Trust, although
the Seadogs have fallen further
than many reformed teams and,
after one promotion, currently
play in the Northern Counties
East Football League Premier
Division, groundsharing with
neighbours Bridlington. **pi**

SUPPORTER OWNERSHIP

THE FALLEN OF THE TRUST MOVEMENT

GARY ANDREWS

MARCH 10TH 2010

THE CURRENT IMPRESSION in this series on supporter ownership is that Trusts or fan ownership largely works. If that were the case, perhaps Exeter wouldn't be an isolated example. As Brian Burgess of Brentford has said, a lot depends on luck and the people you get involved with the Trust. Without decent people on board, the best-meaning business is liable to fail.

Trust-run clubs are also subject to the same financial constraints as other clubs, often more so given how reliant they are on membership. To contrast, this season Charlton Athletic's directors have put in £7 million to the club to fund their push for promotion. Exeter City's Trust has put in £1 million over five years. And with football very much a short-term immediate results driven business,

Trust-run clubs will inevitably come under the same pressures to deliver.

Perhaps one of the saddest examples of this in recent years is at Notts County. The focus of recent months has been, rightly, on Munto, the consortium that took over the club and turned out to be based on thin air and British businessmen rather than rich Arabs. But what can easily be forgotten is that Munto was handed the keys to County by the previous owners, the Supporters' Trust.

We've covered the financial disasters of County's history before on Pitch Invasion, but it's worth quickly summarising how the league's oldest club could go from fan ownership to a smoke and mirrors consortium.

The Notts County Trust played a key part in rallying the fans and fundraising in 2003 following Albert Scardino's disastrous reign before unassuming millionaire supporter Hadyn Green stepped in to save the club and take a 49% stake. In 2007, Green donated his shares to the Trust on the agreement that he would be paid £75,000 if the shares were sold on. Four months later, he died.

But the Magpies' Supporters' Trust could never really galvanise the club in the way Exeter or Brentford did. County languished at the wrong end of the League Two table, never quite getting a grip on the finances or ownership. Constant infighting and bitter disputes wore the board down. In April last year Trust chairman Jon Armstrong-Holmes survived a vote of no confidence from the members. It was a club and Trust trapped in inertia.

The Trust, or certainly Armstrong-Holmes, leapt on the offer from Munto Finance two months later and he embarked on a drive to convince Trust members of the value in handing the Trust's 60% shareholding to Munto, describing their guarantees as "cast iron", adding that Munto were among the most honourable people he had ever met. Members overwhelmingly voted for the Munto takeover and to write off the Trust's loans to the club. We all know what happened next.

Perhaps even more depressing, though, is Stockport County, a side that could genuinely cease to exist at the end of this season. When The Hatters won promotion to League One two years ago, they were held up as yet further proof that Trust ownership was producing success. Less than twelve months later they were in administration with debts of £300,000. Since then, they have been operating under a transfer embargo.

The Stockport County Trust purchased the club for just £1 in 2005, but had one huge problem. Brian Kennedy, the millionaire businessman who owned both County and the Sale Sharks rugby team, retained ownership of Edgeley Park, meaning the Hatters saw huge swathes of potential matchday income denied to them. Limited incoming finances and a mounting unpaid tax bill, along with over-spending in the promotion season, led to an inevitably sad conclusion.

County face being thrown out of the league at the end of the season if they are still in administration. At the current time of writing, former Manchester City player Jim Melrose has, apparently, finally had his consortium's bid for the club accepted by the administrators but, after all that's gone on at the club over previous seasons, Hatters fans know not to get their hopes up.

CHERRY PICKING

Finally, a quick mention for Bournemouth, who, for a short-time was a community-owned club after the fans took over to rescue the Cherries in 2007. Here, perhaps, is a classic example of a club that badly needed a blank slate for such a takeover to be successful.

Bournemouth has been a perennial crisis club for over 15 years now and in 2007 the Cherries went into administration with debts of £4 million. A supporter-backed takeover saved the club at the last minute after some serious bucket-rattling, but while the club was in the hands of the community, so was the debt. And it was that legacy that weighed down on the club.

Despite bouncing back at the first attempt in 2003 after relegation from League One the year before, the financial problems were growing and that year Bournemouth had to call in the PFA to help pay players wages. With debts spiraling and the stadium sold and leased back, the clubs members voted in 2007 to change the constitution that prevented any one person owning more than 10% of the club, as Jeff Mostyn and Steve Sly took control at Dean Court.

What followed was administration in February 2008, with the club's debts at around £5.8 million. Bournemouth was hit with a 10 point deduction, followed by a further 17 points the season after. They narrowly avoided relegation to the Conference and this season has been operating under a seemingly endless transfer embargo.

Meanwhile, ownership was passed from pillar to post as a range of bids for the club collapsed at the last minute before the Sport-6 consortium took over, only for events to unwind even quicker as the debts mounted up. Munto Finance were rumoured to be sniffing around at one point.

Despite resigning during the Sport-6 debacle, Mostyn is still involved with the club as part of a fresh consortium, while ex-Dorchester Town chairman Eddie Mitchell is now the Cherries new chair. Mitchell claims to have reduced the debt from £1.8 million to £800,000 since taking charge, but financial details are thin on the ground. Meanwhile, the club faces yet another winding up order. Some jobs, it seems, are beyond both supporter owners or would-be white knights.

THE FAN WHO TOOK OVER FROM THE TRUST

But not every former Trust-owned club is in dire straits, even if the move away from Trust ownership has been controversial. York City were saved by their Trust in 2003 after former chairman John Batchelor had comprehensively asset-stripped the Minstermen. Many members battled heroically to keep their club alive as a team that had been through so much finally came home to its fans.

But since 2006, York City has been under the ownership of JM Packing, who own 75% of the shares, with the Trust holding the remaining 25%. The company is the family business of Jason McGill and his sister Sophie, dyed in the wool York supporters and active members of the Trust's rescue effort back in 2003.

McGill became chairman but three years later argued that the Trust could no longer take the club forward as well as a professionally backed business and made an offer to buy a majority stake in York. Certainly the club was struggling

at the time, with relegation to the Conference North a possibility. Under the terms of the deal, JM Packing would put in £1 million a year for five years as loans.

When the club sells their ground, Bootham Crescent, as it is contractually bound to do within nine years under the terms of a £2 million loan from the Football Foundation, repayment of the £1 million principal to JM Packaging will be waived. But they will still receive the interest on their loan.

Supporters were divided at the time, but plans for the stadium remain on track and York are looking like genuine contenders for promotion back to the Football League this season. Should York get promotion, a new stadium and secure future, then the JM Packaging takeover may seem like an astute piece of business, while the Trust still retain a piece of ownership.

THE ODD EXPERIMENT

For all the achievements that Trust run clubs have had, as well as their respective failures, the club that has probably generated the most column inches with regard to fan ownership is Ebbsfleet United. Ebbsfleet is definitely not a Trust-run club, but could easily edge towards that model if the will was there.

Despite the blaze of publicity that greeted MyFootballClub.co.uk when they brought Fleet, it's debatable whether you could describe Ebbsfleet as fan-owned currently.

The idea was a simple one: members would sign up to MyFC for £35 a year. The website would then buy a club, funded via the subscriptions, and members would vote on everything from the playing budget to the kit to transfers to picking the team. In theory, it was a footballing utopia; an antidote to the Premier League. In reality, it has been somewhat of a car crash.

Currently MyFC's membership, after the latest round of renewals, stands at just over 4,000, down from a high of 32,000 in February 2008, and down from around 9,000 members this time last year. You don't need a degree in maths to work out that this leaves the Fleet with a serious funding shortfall.

In reality, MyFC's proposition was always going to be a risky venture for Fleet, albeit not for the owner, former journalist Will Brooks. Yes, the cash from the takeover was badly needed by a financially struggling club and,

yes, Ebbsfleet won the FA Trophy soon after the takeover, but those are rare high points.

The problem with MyFC is taking a bunch of fans who have no loyalty to the club, promising them too much (picking the team and other innovations), failing to deliver but still budgeting for a decent number of renewals (and this budget can only be done on a yearly basis, making long-term planning difficult). As the membership has dwindled so have the Fleet's fortunes on and off the pitch.

Tellingly, the current number of MyFC subscriptions is higher than many Trust memberships, including Exeter. But Exeter are in a much more stable financial position, annual losses notwithstanding, than Fleet, which suggests a successful Trust-run club is more than just letting fans run the club — it goes deeper than that. Trust members do not pick the team nor sign the players, or any other gimmick, but they do have a huge say in the way their club is run, democratically. And there lies the difference. **pi**

THE ISRAELI TRUST MOVEMENT

IT'S ALL ABOUT THE COMMUNITY

SHAY GOLUB

SEPTEMBER 14TH 2010

THE ISRAELI SUPPORTERS' trust movement (yes, there is such a thing!) is part of a growing network promoting sustainable clubs through community and fan ownership across Europe. As many will know, Supporters Direct – the body responsible for growing much of this network – began a decade ago in Britain. It is now a movement that is establishing itself successfully across the rest of Europe, including in Israel.

CLUBS IN ISRAEL

From the very first days of the state of Israel (and even before), sport clubs were established in affiliation with political parties and ideological agendas, and up until the early 90s club ownership was highly politically oriented. The major examples were Hapoel clubs associated with the labor movement and Maccabi clubs associated with the Zionist movement.

In the early '90s, the Israeli Football Association (IFA) relocated to UEFA's European confederation, after previously playing in the Asian Football Confederation (AFC) and then the Oceania Football Federation (OFC). The move to European affiliation and to UEFA's competitions started to create an atmosphere for change.

A seemingly dramatic change in the ownership and management of football clubs began to take place: from the politically affiliated associations, which were run by diverse groups of people, connected with vast and various groups in the Israeli society, to private ownership.

At first, the supporters were in favour of this privatisation of their clubs: no more political corruption, but professional clubs with a guaranteed budget that would help them improve their chances in UEFA competitions. Or so they thought.

However, slowly but surely familiar problems related to private ownership started popping up. First, ticket prices increased dramatically, leading to a decrease in the number of fans attending the games. Later, a new law gave the police more responsibilities at the grounds, which led to even more repression of the fans. Above all, the gap between the clubs and their fans was widening.

To be a football fan in Israel has become an almost masochistic pursuit. Football clubs are run by single owners without consideration of the fans and as a result the stadia are empty.

In other countries as well, clubs often refuse to have a dialogue with fans and are run on the basis that clubs are simply 'businesses'. Yet there is usually some sort of acknowledgment that there are fans out there who support the club – not so in Israel.

As a result, there has long been a lot of frustration amongst fans, and a rather depressing mood amongst those in the grounds, as well as the many who don't even bother watching their clubs anymore.

In 2006, in face of this deteriorating situation, Israfans, the Israeli sport supporters' association, was officially established. Most interestingly, following thorough research conducted by the organisation, a very interesting fact was uncovered: the clubs never actually were privatised!

In fact, most of the clubs were still largely funded by direct and indirect governmental sources. The research also found that most of the problems supporters were having were a result of ownership issues and the fact that the voice of the supporters was not (and still isn't) listened to when the clubs are making their decisions, like selling the home ground or changing kick-off times.

ESTABLISHING SUPPORTERS' TRUSTS

The supporters responded with a positive counter-attack and set up supporters' clubs and supporters' trusts. This was done in something of a hybrid version between British-style supporters' trusts (along the models suggested by Supporters Direct) and the German Fan Projects' social programmes. Supporters' trusts aim to serve as an instrument to increase the involvement of supporters in the running of their clubs, ideally gaining ownership, while addressing and involving the whole community. The German Fan Projects, on the other hand, aim to develop the supporters' communities through social work to bring in the community in active and interesting ways.

In the beginning of 2010, a pilot project was established with Hapoel Petach Tikva Supporters Union, a club in the Israeli Premier League, in collaboration with Israfans, the Hothouse, a local youth centre, and the Jewish Distribution Committee (JDC) foundation. The Trust, whose board was composed of various supporter representatives, consulted with Israfans' social advisor for several months and developed a set of tools that built on both the supporters' trust and fan project models.

The toolkit involved social tools like developing a vision for the trust, social marketing and long-term planning, as well as lectures about similar initiatives from around the world.

One of the outcomes of the development stage was "The Youth Project". The Trust took the youth teams of the club under their wing and offered them a series of lectures about the club's importance, and arranged meetings between the youth players and the board of the club – overall, not the typical behavior of an Israeli club.

The project was so successful and received so much support that from next season on it will be implemented in the entire youth department of Hapoel Petah Tikva and in six other cities. In addition, the trust set up a handball and basketball team.

The Hapoel Tikva Supporters Trust was the first of its kind in Israel, but many have been established since: Now Israfans represents six supporters' trusts, three supporter owned clubs and 25 other supporter clubs.

Today, we can talk confidently of a growing supporters' movement in Israel, and Israfans will continue to help develop and grow, assisting trusts in achieving their goals of greater openness and transparency in clubs, along with representation in the running of their clubs. Beyond this, Israfans continues to lobby the IFA and Ministry of Sport to further these objectives.

The growing number of supporters' trusts in Israel show that the number of responsible

supporters who are not happy
with the way their club is run
has grown and resulted in action.
Above all, these fans want to
ensure their clubs continue to
exist and want to be able to support their club.

What they recognise is that in
order to achieve this, the ownership structure of clubs has to
change and football clubs need to
be more transparent and democratically run. **pi**

FROM LEIGH RMI TO LEIGH GENESIS

CHRIS TAYLOR

JUNE 20ᵀᴴ 2008

'VISIONARY CHAIRMAN', WHEN used in a football context, is a troubling little phrase. It's widely accepted that chairmen know if not absolutely nothing about football, then next to nothing. Stick the word 'visionary' in front of them, and it's panic stations time. Football has been around a long time. Most of the important revolutions and evolutions have occurred – crossbars, substitutions, the balti pie: what's left is just tinkering. Yet these supposed visionaries come in, with their mad-cap ideas and hair-brained schemes, and mess everything up for everyone.

You may think that this is the view of a footballing Luddite. A sporting Cro-Magnon man sheltering in his cave, terrified of progress. But it isn't. Change is good. I crave change. But change for the sake of change is crap. Undeniably a bad thing.

In the past, backing up my point, have been visionaries such as Pete Winkleman. He decided to up and move Wimbledon to Milton Keynes? Why? Because he was a visionary and that's what visionaries do. Then there's John Batchelor, who bought York City, changed the team name, the kit design and the badge to reflect his own ego, and then left the club virtually bankrupt, while he made a tidy little profit. And for what reason? Because he was a forward thinking revolutionary who craved and demanded progress. He surfaced again recently when he attempted to buy Mansfield Town, and rename them Harchester United, the fictional team from Sky TV's 'Dream Team' series. Harchester had a greater television presence, and therefore a greater chance of making him loads and loads of money.

So yeah, you'll excuse me if the words 'visionary chairman' fill me with a mixture of dread and perverse fascination. What the devil will these idiots think of next?

Well, ladies and gentlemen, I give you Leigh Genesis.

Last week, Leigh RMI, formerly Horwich RMI, finally dropped the RMI suffix and re-branded as Leigh Genesis. I won't go in to the complicated and long history of Horwich RMI, but it's out there on Wikipedia if you're interested. But in 1995, they moved the seven miles from Horwich to Leigh to give themselves a better chance of making it to the Football League. 13 years on, they still haven't. In fact they're worse off now than they were when they made the move. It was a move that caused many fans to retrospectively call the team 'the original MK Dons'. It was change for change's sake.

RMI, a rather splendid little suffix, stands (stood?) for Railway Mechanics Institute. It hung round the neck of the new club like a train shaped albatross. "There isn't even a train station in Leigh" whined the fans, as if this somehow not only precipitated the need for change, but justified it. Well, I hate to break it to you, my Leigh dwelling chums, but neither is there a Phil Collins prog-rock act. But we don't see you going off on one about that.

The press release announcing the change made for incredible reading. The opening gambit alone had me falling off my comfortable, blue, swivel chair in shock and awe.

"Recently appointed, visionary Chairman Dominic Speakman, 32, explains the thought process behind this radical move to give the club an all-embracing brand for the future."

An all-embracing brand for the future? What does this even mean? It didn't stop there, however. Filling the press release with terms such as 'ideas of colour', 'core of the new brand', 'The alignment of football to fashion' and 'a contemporary edge and is unique in the world of football' gave the impression that the unspeakable Speakman knew exactly what he was doing. But even a casual read revealed that the whole thing was meaningless. It was a classic puff piece of spin and hyperbole. Nothing had any substance. The whole thing was vapid and, frankly, offensive.

I was obviously furious. Speakman was essentially trampling over history and removing any trace he could find of the previous club, Horwich RMI. By creating a new club, in a new stadium, in new colours, he has formed a new team half way up the pyramid. The only thing that links Leigh RMI and Speakenstein's Monster is the town in which they're based.

Initially, people – thankfully – seemed as up in arms about this I as was. As far as I could tell it was seen as a travesty, and another case of football eating itself. Message boards (OK, maybe I was naïve taking Internet forums as proof of anything other than there being a scary, scary world outside my front door) were full of debate and comment about how this was a terrible thing. I posted a blog entry about it, expecting messages of condemnation for Speakman and Leigh Genesis, but instead got something rather different.

It seems the people of Leigh are fully behind this move. Not one 'Genesis' fan I have spoken to has anything other than a good word for Speakman and his new club. Apart from those who have a very bad word for me. A very bad word indeed. They are genuinely excited by the fresh start, and the opportunity to progress. They have been blinded by the promise of a better future, and perhaps aren't thinking critically enough about it.

Leigh Genesis, apart from the re-branding, will be playing professionally next season. They are, as far as I know, the lowest placed team in the football pyramid to be doing so. I can think of two other teams who attempted this at Northern Premier League level, Grantham Town and Colne Dynamoes. Grantham have only just regained a sound financial footing a decade later, and Colne Dynamoes folded in 1990. There just isn't the fan base and money at that level to support a professional team. But what does history know when up against a 'visionary chairman'?

Leigh will take to the field in August, and everyone will be rosy-cheeked and optimistic about the future. And while I hope Speakman gets his legs kicked out from under him – let's not forget he's the real bad guy in all this – I don't wish any ill whatsoever on the fans. I'm disappointed they're so thoroughly behind this abomination, but hey, that's the beauty of football. Differing views, personal choice, it's all part of the rich tapestry of life.

No. What I'm really angry about is that this is another

example of football being allowed to destroy itself. We're stuck in a vicious circle with this type of name changing and club moving. The more commonplace it becomes, the more acceptable it will appear to people. And the more people accept it, the more it will happen in the future. And while Leigh fans may be delighted with Speakman and his new start, others in the future probably won't be so lucky. **pi**

THOSE JARI VIITA PEOPLE

EGAN RICHARDSON

MAY 5TH 2009

ARI HJELM HAS been with Tampere United throughout their ten-year history, first as an assistant to Harri Kampman and then from 2001 as head coach. He has won three championships, and it is a common refrain in Tampere that he is primarily responsible for the club's success, and that he is the best coach in the country. He has now seen off his enemies in the club, after last week's departure of Sporting Director Jarkko Wiss and Chief Executive Sami Salonen, and is the master of all he surveys. Rightly so, argue many in Tampere, as he is the most successful coach the city has ever produced.

This argument is often advanced in the city's pubs, and so it was one evening last October when a man wanted to talk football with me. Conversation turned to the coaching situation in Finland, and the man's stridently expressed opinion that Hjelm is the best coach in the country.

The dialogue meandered around a bit, with me slightly sceptical about Hjelm's qualities, until I offered the opinion that maybe Jarkko Wiss would one day make a good coach. The man snorted. That's not poetic licence – it was an actual, beer spraying snort.

"I see. So you're one of those people. Those Jari Viita people," came the explanation for his derision.

My interlocutor wanted to drum home the point that TamU was Hjelm and Hjelm was TamU, and it seemed to him as though the battle lines were drawn and

Tampere football was divided into two groups: the Hjelm supporters and the rest. With us or against us. Hjelm was under pressure, as Juha Koskimäki and Kalevi Salonen – two key Hjelm allies within the club – had been fired by TamU chairman Viita, and the team's performance had been poor.

"I'm sad that so much know-how has left this club," Hjelm told STT after Koskimäki and Salonen's departures in October 2008. "Neither me nor Ari Hjelm had any say in the team's affairs," sacked manager Salonen chimed in. "Zico (Hjelm) has not been able to decide who to play in the team and who to leave out, everything has been decided by Jari Viita and Jarkko Wiss. This has been going on for a long time, since the turn of the year."

Viita had wanted to sack Hjelm after a 5-1 defeat at HJK early in the season, but was persuaded that this was unwise by other directors. The expense of paying off Hjelm's recently signed two year contract was a big factor in the decision, because fundamental differences over strategy were beginning to show themselves in the team's performance and it was clear even then that big changes needed to be made in the club's management structure.

Hjelm fought back, complaining in the tabloids about the loss of Juska Savolainen and the poor quality replacements, but a TamU director vehemently insisted to me at the time that Hjelm had approved all transfer dealings and requested all the players TamU had signed after the 2007 season.

Jari Viita became involved with Tampere United during one of their periodic financial crises, when he bought shares to cover a budget shortfall. Also owner of the magnificently named Riihimäen Cocks handball team, he is still one of the major shareholders in Tampere United, and along with English businessman Tim Rowe and ice hockey power broker Kalervo Kummola has held a major stake and put money in at crucial times during the club's history.

Wiss's role was similarly important. After retirement in 2007, he became TamU's Sporting Director with responsibility for player recruitment, and Hjelm and his long-standing friends and colleagues were pushed aside from the buying and selling of players and negotiation of contracts. Hjelm has always had a difficult relationship with his bosses, and adding a valued former player to the mix was, in hindsight, always likely to be difficult for him to accept.

The idea was that Wiss's contacts, international experience and language skills would provide the club with better value signings, which would save the club money and enable them to progress to compete regularly in Europe, preferably in the group stages of the Champions League.

Part of the plan was the TamU academy team, which was to compete initially in the winter SM Liiga series. The idea of this team was to draw the best players from all the Tampere clubs – which have historically been at loggerheads for many reasons, among them political ones – and give them quality training three times a week at Tampere's sport high school.

When the idea was mooted, a lot of Tampere's young prospects were playing in the lower divisions of the Finnish youth structure, and the TamU academy would give them a chance to play against better players, train as an elite group of Tampere's best young talents, and provide an easier access point for the national team coaches.

Similarly, the academy was intended to attract young players from outside of Tampere, and Johannes Mononen was one of the first to sign, moving to Tampere

from the North Karelian town of Joensuu at the age of just 17.

Revenue from transferring young players to bigger European teams would establish Tampere United as Finland's pre-eminent club, draw more fans, increase sponsorship revenue, and change the rules of engagement in Finnish football.

In principle, the plan was flawless. While Ari Hjelm has achieved some fantastic results, with three championships to his name, he is rarely seen at lower league matches in Tampere, where younger players are frequently scouted. In 2007, Inter Turku signed 21-year-old midfielder Severi Paajanen from Tampere side PP-70, for instance. Meanwhile, TamU bought 30-year-old Antti Pohja from HJK.

This is the kind of move that wins championships, but costs a lot of money, and when pursued as part of a strategy can be indicative of a short term outlook. The academy was supposed to provide an alternative, a direct route for the best young players in Tampere into Tampere United's first team, but with Wiss leaving the club, the academy is likely to be mothballed. Academy coach Tomi Jalkanen has already tendered his resignation, although TamU's press officer was not able to confirm his departure at the time of writing.

Hjelm's friends are long-standing bigwigs of the Tampere football scene. The club was born from the bankruptcy of Ilves in 1998, and along with Ari Hjelm they also took Juha Koskimäki from the defunct club.

Koskimäki had been TamU's team director, and Kalevi Salonen the manager (he had filled a similar role with the other big Tampere club, TPV), until they were fired last October. They performed those undefined backroom roles that allow many people to be 'involved' in Finnish football, but their real function was clear: bringing in the sponsor money from their friends among the local business community.

This function is crucial in Finland. Most teams rely on sponsorship money almost to the exclusion of all other income streams, as attendances are so low, and the ability to press the flesh among the sponsors is highly prized by Finnish clubs.

The power brokers in Finnish sport sponsorship are usually middle aged men, and the clubs usually choose middle aged men to buttress these relationships.

Koskimäki and Salonen have been TamU's sponsorship rainmakers, and notwithstanding Koskimäki's role in Ilves's bankruptcy, they had helped ensure the smooth flow of sponsorship money into the club.

Funding a club via one or two main sponsors, or via gate money generated by a large fanbase, is unheard of for these guys. They were brought up in the Finnish football tradition, where the sponsor is king and the fan unimportant. The shortcomings of Ratina Stadium (it is far too big and the fans are remote from the pitch) are overlooked by many who share this worldview, because it provides better VIP facilities for sponsors than the second stadium in Tampere, Tammela.

These Finnish sponsorship deals are simple. The sponsors get exposure on the shirt or in the ground, and the freedom to consume as much potato salad, mustamakkara, cider and beer as they can at each and every home game. It's an arrangement that suits them, as the sponsorship cost can be written off against VAT and, well, everyone likes beer and mustamakkara, right?

Back in October, the man in the bar was explaining all this, and the fact that TamU would now find it difficult to get sponsorship revenue without Koskimäki and Salonen. That small circles of people can have such an influence on one of Finland's most successful football clubs without actually putting that much money in, just one year after the club filled Ratina Stadium for a Champions League tie against Rosenborg, is a reflection on the missed opportunities that could have led to a new, brighter future.

In the wake of the Rosenborg game the club was looking to capitalise on the publicity. Ticket prices went up, sponsorship became more expensive, and there was a real drive to make TamU the third force in the city, after the Ilves and Tappara hockey clubs. The scourge of the Finnish football shirt – a thousand logos making the players look like clowns – could have been dealt with, and it was hoped that fewer sponsors would contribute more money, and make the organisation more professional.

This failed for a number of reasons, and the level at which sponsorships were offered was a source of friction within Tampere United: the more professionally minded people in the organisation wanted to take advantage of TamU's position as one of the leading clubs in the country, while the old guard did not want to squeeze the sponsors – who are, essentially, their mates – too hard. This conflict had a generational dimension too. The new guard, personified by Sami Salonen and Jarkko Wiss, are internationally minded, young, and see Tampere United as part of a European scene that offers huge revenues in comparison to domestic football. The old guard sees the Finnish championship and local bragging rights as paramount, and usually has another job in addition to a position at a football club.

Jari Viita had left the club in the autumn as his business was in financial difficulties and he could not inject the sums necessary to keep the club ticking over, with Harri Pyhältö taking his place as chairman. The control of sponsorship revenue is effectively control of the club, in the absence of directors subscribing to share issues, but for good measure TamU had found a new shareholder and sponsor in the Kangasala grit and asphalt manufacturer Soraset. The club had no alternative plan, and with revenue drying up there was little alternative but to sell more shares in the club.

This deal was negotiated by Pyhältö – another long-time associate of Hjelm, Koskimäki and Kalevi Salonen – with little input from the club's Chief Executive, Sami Salonen. It gave Soraset an 18% share in Tampere United in return for 220,000 Euros, at a time when the club was in dire need of funds, and added a new ingredient to the power balance that had long fluctuated between Rowe, Viita and Kummola. The way was clear for the return of the old guard.

After Salonen and Koskimäki returned to the club in March, the writing seemed to be on the wall for Wiss and Sami Salonen. Kalevi Salonen's new position on his return was 'special assistant to the chairman', while Juha Koskimäki was the head of the sales group, with the task of selling sponsorship.

At Saturday's game against VPS, TamU figures were tight lipped. Thankfully Jari Viita was not, telling Ilta Sanomat's Jari Perkiö that the departure of Salonen and Wiss and the return of the 'old guard' were unsurprising events for him.

"I completely expected this, I've known for a long time that this would happen. The old guard, led by Ari Hjelm, got what they wanted."

Perkiö asked for a clarification: do you mean that Hjelm is behind this?

"That's correct. We had completely different views on how to develop the club. He wants 25-year-old Finnish players, because he can't communicate in any other languages. We tried to change TamU radically, but we quickly noticed the old guard's intent."

"Maybe it would have been enough for these brats if we'd received a little support from the council. But we didn't get a penny."

Viita was annoyed at the city council on another count, too. Apparently TamU made many proposals to improve the facilities at Ratina, which is owned by the council, but there was never a response.

"And this year tops it all, when they couldn't even provide us with a winter training facility. Nor did they get Ratina into a playable condition by the start of the Veikkausliiga season, even though the weather was good."

"Even if we had the heavenly father as coach and Bill Gates as chairman, under these conditions we would not be successful."

In the midst of all this are the fans. Tampere United have a large and active fans group, who have grown over the last five years to become an integral part of the match day experience. The group is called *Sinikaarti* (Blue Guard), they were established in 2003, and they are unhappy at the way the club has been run.

"These middle-aged guys don't know anything," said one long-standing fan. "They think the club is their own personal property and they don't care about anything else. They don't speak English, they cannot sell players abroad let alone recruit from there, and they look like Swiss Tony."

The resemblance to the Fast Show character is undeniable, at least in Koskimäki's case, and the generational conflict is most sharply apparent where the fans are concerned. They are mainly young, take their cue from the ultra scene in other countries, and they see the opportunities that have been missed in a way that some middle aged Finnish men don't.

At Saturday's game they hung their Sinikaarti banner upside down in the style of dissatisfied ultras from all over Europe, and held a protest before the game which involved a banner reading: "*Ammattimaisuuden puolesta, puuhastelua vastaan! Seurajohto: strategianne?*" This roughly translates as "for professionalism, against unprofessional farting around! Management: what's your strategy?"

They were silent for the first 14 minutes, before chanting 'Wiss!' 14 times in honour of the former captain and latter day Sporting Director's squad number.

This followed a '*Kiitos* Seve' banner at the away game against MyPa, thanking departed CEO Sami 'Seve' Salonen for his work with the club. After the 4-1 defeat, club captain Mikko Kavén led his team over to applaud the fans – something TamU players have occasionally failed to do even when they've won a game – and he was dropped by Ari Hjelm for the match against VPS on Saturday. He is not expected to return to the side any time soon.

Meanwhile, the conspiracy theorists are working overtime. Tampere football has long been divided along political lines, with TPV being the nominally left wing club and Ilves the nominally right wing club. This political dimension shows at matches, where Social Democrat MP Jukka Gustafsson is always present to cheer on TPV.

The Tampere United board is now composed mainly of men formerly linked to Ilves, and the theory goes that they are not too bothered if TamU go bankrupt and get relegated, because they could then sell the league place to the newly reformed Ilves, who are currently playing in the third tier of Finnish football, Kakkonen.

This theory holds that the departures of Salonen and Wiss were necessary because they are not Ilves people: Wiss was a TPV junior, and Salonen previously worked for Tamhockey Oy, the holding company in charge of Tappara, which in turn has an affinity and cooperation deals with TPV.

Whatever the reason – and the most likely explanation is simply that these children just did not want to share 'their' toy – Tampere United will now face a long struggle to return to the heights they had attained during the 2007 Champions League campaign. **pi**

WHAT NEEDS TO CHANGE IN NON-LEAGUE FOOTBALL

DAVE BOYLE

JANUARY 3RD 2008

THE LAST FIVE years as an AFC Wimbledon fan have immersed me in non-League football. Up to then, I thought of non-League in much the same way as many who have not fully experienced it. Corinthian amateurs playing for the love of it, fans united in pursuit of survival rather than unrealistic dreams of global domination, officials motivated by simple service rather than power-brokering and politicking.

There is much of the non-League story about which English football can be justly proud. The depth of competitive football across the country is something that truly marks it out from many, many other countries and that is in no small part thanks to the unpaid hours put in by supporters all over the country. The culture of personal sacrifice, or pitching in for the greater good with no reward other than just making sure a team can take the park and the punters can pay over the turnstile.

But there is another side to the game which is less than admirable. I consider myself a friend of non-League football, and occasionally, friends have to tell people some home truths that might seem harsh. Like friends in our personal lives, I hope that people understand they are motivated by a desire to see the game improve and become what it could so easily be.

THE CHALLENGE OF NON-LEAGUE FOOTBALL

It is important to recognise at the start the obstacles many clubs have to deal with. They are trying to compete against people with better resources, better access to the media and more pull with unaffiliated football fans. There is a justified sense of resentment at the way in which the better appointed within the game seem to go out of their way to make life difficult, such as with the scheduling of European matches.

But the idea that if some things from 'big football' simply disappeared life would become good is both untrue and dangerous. It stops the microscope being turned inwards to see what problems lie there.

For starters, there is a simple reason why non-League topics do not get coverage on national and regional TV or newspapers. Clubs outside the top six in the Premiership can make the same claim, and with more people watching the Football League clubs each year than the Premiership, it is a justified grievance. But below the bottom tier of the Football League, the lack of coverage reflects the reality of the audience's interests, not bias against the non-League game.

Take midweek matches. There is absolutely no chance of the bigger clubs holding a moratorium on week night fixtures. Therefore smaller clubs would

be better advised to try to work out why people prefer their sofas and TV than vainly hoping for the European Cup will revert to its old knock-out format.

Now, I'm sure that some would cite a chicken and egg argument here. The lack of coverage the non-League game gets does contribute to the lack of profile the top flight gets for free in every daily newspaper. But regardless of what came first, the top flight is not going to forego coverage, and nor are the newspapers about to radically reappraise their policy.

CHANGING NON-LEAGUE FOOTBALL

Change is going to have to come from below. And that change might include the 'exclusive' atmosphere that some clubs cultivate. Make no bones about it – following non-League sides is a labour of love. To keep the faith in the face of the rival fayre on offer, the facilities provided and the length of journeys involved requires an uncommon sense of attachment. But maybe this virtue is also a potential problem?

Let me explain. If football fandom is obsessional, to extend the metaphor, non-League is a little kinky. It is an acquired taste, and like stilton, black olives and real ale, things that need effort to be acquired will always be minority pursuits in competition to the blandness of the mass-market cheddars and lagers.

But in an environment where the very existence of a club is permanently in doubt, what tastes are people being invited to acquire?

THE SIEGE MENTALITY

When some Manchester United fans intimated they were thinking of starting their own team (ultimately FC United of Manchester), many in non-League criticised them. Why did they not all start watching nearby Altrincham or Droylsden? The point is that the whole reason they wanted to start again was because they were annoyed at having someone steal their club. The last thing they wanted was to do the same to others.

More cynically, officials of one club effectively offered to sell FC United their league place in the Conference as long as they played in that town, an offer the FC United board immediately refused. At AFC Wimbledon, some long-standing officials of Kingstonian intimated that a merger between the two clubs would make most sense.

Sadly, the fans of both FC United and AFC Wimbledon continue to be on the end of grumpy letters in the *Non-League Paper* and on various internet fora. The main crime they appear to have committed, though, is simply to be new. They have not got the battle scars from flirting with extinction, nor the enamel badges of the glorious F.A. Trophy run to the semi-finals way back in the day.

Through my day job I have been lucky enough to travel the country working with fans at the 45 non-League clubs who now have a Supporters' Trust, and through Wimbledon I have seen a lot more clubs.

At many clubs there is something there that looks very much like a siege mentality. There seems to be a lingering passive-aggressive sense that everyone is being measured by how much – or how little – they are doing for the cause. Are they a real fan? Do they do enough?

Let's imagine you have moved to an area with a small non-League club. You don't want to go to the professional club up the road; you like the idea of non-League football and you're attracted to a place without the exploitative attitude prevalent higher up the leagues.

You'll find that the price to get in will more than likely be over £10, which surprises you, as the place looks and feels ramshackle. The toilets are pretty basic and you might see fixtures and fittings well past their useful life, victims of one-too-many cutbacks on year-end maintenance having to be shelved through lack of funds.

You'll be asked to add to your spending for a burger that is often unedifying and potentially unhealthy. There is the commemorative badge to buy, the collection of old programmes to peruse, the Race Night to go to, the end of season fundraiser to turn out for. There is an all-pervading sense of this club having to practically suck money out of people over and above the basics of a match ticket and a cup of tea.

So you contribute but wonder why, despite this, the club seems to be living hand-to-mouth and whether things could perhaps be improved on the cost control side of things, with every bill a crisis waiting to explode. You are told – like an article of faith – that the board and the officials are tremendous chaps who work ever so hard and have done for years. The fact that the benefits of their efforts

are not particularly clear is neither here nor there.

The Supporters' Club often do not seem interested as there is a raffle to organise, and ultimately one would not want to annoy the directors by asking difficult questions. What if they stop the players attending the end-of-the-season function organised by the Supporters' Club? The whole thing feels like a fund-raising scheme that occasionally plays a match and you would be forgiven for deciding that it is not for you.

Best keep to oneself darker thoughts about rampant egos of many of the people who have become owners or chairmen of non-League clubs, musings about why people are prepared to get involved in this level, about the status of the loans the board makes, and whether the ground might be being lined up for redevelopment.

THE ENDLESS CRISIS

It has been going on so long that many simply accept this as the natural order of things. Every few years, the budgets get blasted apart, a crisis ensues, and new local worthies come forward. They run the club the same way as their predecessors, the debts build up and there is a crisis again a bit later leading to a new set of worthies coming forward. Repeat again and again, with a ground sale and new stadium thrown in every generation or so.

Except each time, a little bit more of the club dies. A few more supporters disappear, and a few other potential fans walk away. And a strategy for success that seems to be based on importing the worst features of the professional game will never resolve it.

There is a palpable sense that so many clubs are so desperate for success, so desperate for an end to the incessant work and fundraising that they will be grateful for any benefactor in a storm, who often as not will leave a few years hence. To paraphrase the Life of Brian, fans say "you're the saviour of the club, and we should know, since we've followed a few!"

The days when non-League football could regularly get five-figure crowds have gone, as have the clubs who were best placed to get those types of crowds, most of them having become league clubs over the last 40 years.

COMMUNITY CLUBS

The only path to success for non-League clubs is to truly re-orientate themselves as community clubs: owned by their communities and run by them, not by an assorted collection of businessmen of dubious strategic vision, nor giants of the local football scene who have been doing it their way for so long that they have forgotten that new ideas are always needed. All of this is, of course, dependent on a volunteer army of well-meaning fans who have for too long acted as though it is tantamount to treason to ask that their love and loyalty be rewarded with a meaningful stake in the club, and a say in how it is run.

Non-League football – away from the hype and greed of the professional game – is well placed to enjoy a renaissance as people want to see their local club and be filled with pride at being able to identify as a supporter of it. As fans of AFC Wimbledon and FC United of Manchester have shown, people who have enjoyed the Premiership can find a lot more to cherish further down.

But for it to happen, the current generation have to change the vibe. There are good times waiting to happen across the country if supporters can grasp the opportunity to make it happen and take on real involvement themselves. Time to get the party started! **pi**

EDITOR

Tom Dunmore is the founder of Pitch Invasion. He is the author of the Historical Dictionary of Soccer, published by Scarecrow Press in September 2011. Tom can be followed on Twitter @pitchinvasion.

CONTRIBUTORS

Gary Andrews is a freelance football writer and broadcast journalist. He has written for When Saturday Comes, the BBC and ITV and co-hosts the twofootedtackle.com podcast. He has a particular interest in fan ownership and lower league football and is a long-suffering Exeter City supporter.

Marc Bahnsen is from Chicago where he lives and works for the beautiful game. On the weekend he has been known to imbibe tea and whiskey while tending to his concrete garden.

Dave Boyle worked for Supporters Direct from 2000 to 2011, the UK-based group developing greater supporter involvement in sports clubs, the last three years as chief executive. He is now a consultant and writer, and blogs at www.dave-boyle.net and is on twitter @theboyler.

Bobby Brandon is a blogger from Charlotte, North Carolina. He can be reached at bobbybrandon@gmail.com.

Jennifer Doyle teaches in the English Department at the University of California, Riverside. Since 2007, she has blogged as From a Left Wing. Jennifer is currently writing a book on the "athletic gesture" in sport and in visual art. She lives and plays in Los Angeles.

Zach Dundas cut his teeth as a soccer fan as part of a six-person "ultras" section at University of Montana women's games in the '90s. He now lives and works in the post-modern football hotbed of Portland, where he suffers for past sins at the hands of the Portland Timbers and the Liverpool Football Club. His first book, The Renegade Sportsman, includes an extended essay on the nature of American soccer fandom.

Shay Golub is the chair of Israfans, the Israeli National Sport supporters organization and a campaign manager. He lectures about Jewish soccer before World War Two and supports Hapoel Kfar Saba.

Andrew Guest is an academic social scientist and soccer addict living in Portland, Oregon. Having worked (and played) in Malawi and Angola, he has a particular interest in Africa. He's also interested in the psychology and sociology of sport, and is always looking for interesting ways to engage and enjoy the game.

Mike Innes continues to run the Go! Go! Omiya Ardija fan site.

Michał Karaś is the editor-in-chief of Stadiony.net, a Polish website dedicated to football stadiums. Michał is a Jagiellonian University graduate, MA in journalism, enthusiast of supporter culture and sports architecture, but most of all a Wisla Krakow fan.

David Keyes is a PhD student in the Department of Anthropology at the University of California, San Diego. His research focuses on the growth of youth soccer in the U.S. in the post-World War Two period and the relationship between soccer in the Anglo and Latino communities.

Benjamin Kumming is a writer of fiction and non-fiction living in Chicago. When not ruing his fate in the beautiful game, he can be found at benjaminkumming.com.

Jack Lord teaches and studies African history at the School of Oriental and African Studies, University of London. His research, almost none of which is about football, can be found at http://soas.academia.edu/JackLord

JL Murtaugh is originally from Chicago, now based in London, and maintains jlmurtaugh.com and nogrand.co.uk.

Supriya Nair is a journalist and AC Milan fan in Bombay, India. She can be followed on Twitter @supriyan.

Brian Phillips is the editor of The Run of Play and a staff writer at Grantland. His work has appeared in Slate, Deadspin, and the New York Times Magazine, among other publications.

Egan Richardson is a journalist and broadcaster based in Helsinki. He works for the Finnish state broadcaster YLE, among others, and divides his spare time between Finnish lower division football and following Sheffield Wednesday.

Chris Taylor is a vigilante from the North West of England. The self-styled Joey Barton of prose, he can usually be found in Nando's eating the piri-piri half chicken platter, drinking super bock, and reading Orwell's Keep The Aspidistra Flying.

Mike Tuckerman is a columnist for The Roar, an Australian sports website.

Alex Usher is a consultant in higher education policy and management, but secretly wishes he was Jonathan Wilson instead. For his sins, he supports Toronto FC.

Richard Whittall is the editor of theScore Channel's Footy Blog. His work has appeared in the Globe and Mail and Toronto Life. Richard can be followed on Twitter @rwhittall.

Vanda Wilcox teaches modern European history at John Cabot University in Rome, where she has lived since 2006. She supports Roma and Lodigiani in Italy but still has feelings for Arsenal. As well as historical research on the First World War in Italy and Italian national identity she has published articles on Italian fan culture, and is currently working on a book about the ultras movement.

Peter Wilt has run professional soccer teams for 25 years and has won six championship rings, including four with the Chicago Fire, in three professional soccer leagues. He likes to write about soccer, history and people. Peter is on Twitter @PeterWilt1.

CPSIA information can be obtained at www.ICGtesting.com
Printed in the USA
BVOW031109060312

284553BV00001B/61/P